Prayers and Practices for the Souls in Purgatory

By Fr. Dan Cambra, MIC,
with Andrew Leeco

Available from:
Marian Helpers Center
Stockbridge, MA 01263
1-800-462-7426
marian.org
ShopMercy.org

ISBN: 978-1-59614-407-1

Imprimi Potest:
Very Rev. Kazimierz Chwalek, MIC, Provincial Superior
The Blessed Virgin Mary, Mother of Mercy Province
Congregation of Marian Fathers of the Immaculate Conception
July 17, 2017

Nihil Obstat:
Dr. Robert A. Stackpole, STD
Censor Deputatus
July 17, 2017

Acknowledgements:
Dave Came, Andrew Leeco, Felix Carroll, Chris Sparks,
Mary Clark, Tad Floridis, and Fr. Chris Alar, MIC,
without whom this book would not have happened.
I am grateful to God for all the blessings I have received as
a priest, a Marian, a Catholic, and a Christian.

Dedicated to

*St. Stanislaus of Jesus and Mary Papczynski, our
Founder; to my novice master, Fr. Tim Roth, MIC,
who was my first Marian teacher; Br. Andrew
Maczynski, MIC, the Very Rev. Fr. Kazimierz
Chwalek, MIC, and all those who helped bring
about St. Stanislaus' canonization in our day; and
Fr. Donald Petraitis, MIC, Fr. Victor Rimselis, MIC,
and Fr. Mark Garrow, MIC, whose wisdom
and love continue to guide me.*

CONTENTS

INTRODUCTION

I first learned about the Holy Souls in Purgatory when I was maybe 5 or 6 years old. I would sometimes hear somebody either knocking at my bedroom door or even calling my name. I'd get up and go look to see who was calling my name.

I wouldn't find anyone.

At that time, my great-grandmother was my babysitter because both of my parents and all four of my grandparents worked.

I asked my great-grandmother if she had knocked.

She said, "No."

I asked her if she had called my name.

No, she hadn't called my name. She said to me, "That's probably the poor souls in Purgatory who want you to say a prayer for them, so say three Hail Marys for them and go back to sleep." So whenever I heard a knock or someone calling my name to wake me up, I assumed it was the poor souls asking for my prayers. So I'd say three Hail Marys and go back to sleep.

As I grew older, my devotion to the souls in Purgatory also grew. When I was in the process of discerning a religious life, I looked at more than 45 different communities. Ultimately, it came down to a choice between two. At the last minute, I made a retreat with the Marian Fathers, and for the first time in my life, I discovered a religious community that offered prayers every day for the Holy Souls in Purgatory. I found out that it was part of the spirituality of the Marians' Father Founder, St. Stanislaus Papczynski, to pray for the souls in Purgatory, especially those for whom no one ever prayed. Well, that matched the spirituality I had learned from my great-grandmother and practiced since childhood, so when I encountered the same focus on the Holy Souls in the Marians, it really struck me rather strongly. It was one of the main reasons why I decided to become a Marian. Praying for the Holy Souls in Purgatory was foundational to my choice of vocation.

And my devotion has continued to deepen through the years. I am always seeking out new prayers and practices as I pray for these suffering souls. For instance, after meeting Immaculee

Ilibagiza, the well-known survivor of the Rwandan genocide and devotee of Our Lady of Kibeho, I now say the Chaplet of the Seven Sorrows of Mary every Friday for the souls in Purgatory, and every day during Lent. Immaculee recommended this chaplet to me, and I'm glad I took her up on the recommendation. It's a particularly touching devotion for me, and a powerful means of making reparation for sins, requesting the grace to continue to leave behind vice, and receiving the strength to grow in virtue.

The fact that you're reading this book says that you too are looking to help the Holy Souls, either as a newcomer to the devotion or as someone looking for new practices or more formation in what it means to pray for them. Whether you have been praying for the Holy Souls for as long as I have or are just starting out, I have a suggestion for you: Even the busiest of people can say three Hail Marys each day. I once heard a story about somebody who felt they didn't have time for much in the way of prayer every day, but at least found the time to say three Hail Marys daily for the suffering souls in Purgatory. When this particular person died, he found out that the only thing that kept him out of hell was his charity to these poor souls.

Nowadays, a lot of people have heard my story about the knocks in the middle of the night, so I'm often asked if I still hear the knocks. At this particular point in my life, I don't often hear voices calling me in the night or knocks on the door — God has blessed me instead with other reasons that a middle-aged man needs to get up a couple of times a night. So I still have the opportunity to say those three Hail Marys for the Holy Souls before I fall back into bed.

May this book inspire you to do likewise. I've collected an array of writings by my brother Marian Fathers, Marian Helpers, and myself. Each contribution touches on some key element of the doctrine or devotion surrounding Purgatory, helping you understand what Purgatory is, why it's needed, and how it's a manifestation of Divine Mercy, as well as how to set these captives free and speed the Holy Souls on their road to Heaven. Divine Revelation shows us through Scripture and Tradition that this devotion is so necessary, so important, and such a great work of mercy. I beg of you on behalf of the Holy Souls, take it up,

whether you do as little for them as three Hail Marys a day or as much as Gregorian Masses or daily Rosaries for them. Don't neglect praying for the Holy Souls, and you'll find throughout your life and into eternity that there is no one more grateful than our brethren in Purgatory.

Pray with me now: Eternal rest grant unto them, O Lord, and let perpetual light shine upon them. May their souls and all the souls of the faithful departed, through the mercy of God, rest in peace. Amen.

May Jesus, the Divine Mercy, bless you, and Mary, Star of the Sea, always intercede on your behalf.

Fr. Dan Cambra, MIC
Spiritual Director, *Holy Souls Sodality*

SECTION 1

SCRIPTURE
and
TRADITION

Chapter 1
THE BASICS

What is Purgatory?

Purgatory is the state of those who die in God's friendship, assured of their eternal salvation, but who still have need of purification to enter into the happiness of Heaven.

Saint Catherine of Genoa says that, although Purgatory is incomparably painful because we see all the horror of our own sins, it is also incomparably joyful because God is with us there, where we are learning to endure His truth and His light (see *Treatise on Purgatory*). It is also joyful because all those in Purgatory have already passed through particular judgment (the judgment of Christ on their souls when they die) and are assured of their eventual entrance into Heaven.

How do we know Purgatory exists?

The existence of Purgatory logically follows from two facts: our imperfection on earth and our perfection in Heaven.

Of the "Final Purification, or Purgatory," the *Catechism of the Catholic Church* (1031) teaches:

> The Church gives the name *Purgatory* to this final purification of the elect, which is entirely different from the punishment of the damned (Cf. Council of Florence (1439): DS 1304; Council of Trent (1563): DS 1820; (1547): 1580; see also Benedict XII, Benedictus Deus (1336): DS 1000). The Church formulated her doctrine of faith on Purgatory especially at the Councils of Florence and Trent. The tradition of the Church, by reference to certain texts of Scripture, speaks of a cleansing fire (Cf. *1 Cor* 3:15; *1 Pet* 1:7):
>
> > As for certain lesser faults, we must believe that, before the Final Judgment, there is a purifying

fire. He who is truth says that whoever utters blasphemy against the Holy Spirit will be pardoned neither in this age nor in the age to come. From this sentence we understand that certain offenses can be forgiven in this age, but certain others in the age to come (St. Gregory the Great, *Dial.* 4, 39: PL 77, 396; cf. *Mt* 12:31).

We can also know that Purgatory exists through the testimony of Sacred Scripture (see Chapter 2) and Tradition (see Chapter 3), as well as through the eyewitness testimony of saints and mystics (see Chapters 8-10).

Who are the Holy Souls in Purgatory?

Some people die in the grace of God as His friends, but are still imperfect and require a "purification" before entering Heaven. These "Holy Souls" are sent to Purgatory for that purification. We call them "holy" because, although they are not yet perfect, they are on the way to Heaven.

The souls in Purgatory are also called "poor souls" because they are suffering to some extent. That is, they realize they must be purified and are still not in union with God in Heaven (see *Catechism*, 1030-1032).

Why do the Holy Souls need our help?

The Church teaches that the Holy Souls in Purgatory cannot pray for themselves. Think of it this way: While we are living in the world, we must have great faith and practice good works in the hopes of attaining our eternal reward in Heaven. Once we die, we can no longer do this, so we must await purification in Purgatory. The prayers of the living bring these Holy Souls consolation and help in attaining their eternal reward. In Purgatory, where Divine Justice purifies souls, the burning pain of waiting can be extinguished by suffrages — that is, by the prayers and sacrifices of the living.

What can we do to help the Holy Souls?

We can offer our sacrifices, prayers, corporal and spiritual works of mercy, and almsgiving for the release of the Holy Souls. In *Mystical Temple of God* (Marian Press, 2013, p. 116), the Founder of the Marian Fathers, St. Stanislaus Papczynski, says:

> What is appropriate for us to do; for us who can obtain much from Jesus, and have such frequent incentives to bring assistance to the souls of the faithful who are destined for temporary torture? Therefore, I am greatly amazed how it is possible that a Christian does not begin to feel deeply the entreaty of these souls who cry aloud in these words: "Pity me, pity me, O you my friends!" (Jb 19:21). What about the fact that we shall have in heaven as many Patrons and helpers as many souls we have brought there, thanks to our help, from the furnace of purgatory! I do not relate many things on this subject; let it suffice to consider and follow what the Holy Spirit declared: "it is therefore a holy and wholesome thought to pray for the dead, that they may be loosened from sins" (LV 2 Macc 12:45-46).

God allows us this opportunity to be merciful and cooperate with His plan for the salvation for all souls. The *Catechism* (1032) further explains:

> This teaching is also based on the practice of prayer for the dead, already mentioned in Sacred Scripture: "Therefore [Judas Maccabeus] made atonement for the dead, that they might be delivered from their sin" [*2 Macc* 12:46]. From the beginning the Church has honored the memory of the dead and offered prayers in suffrage for them, above all the Eucharistic sacrifice, so that, thus purified, they may attain the beatific vision of God (Cf. Council of Lyons II (1274): DS 856). The Church also commends almsgiving, indulgences, and works of penance undertaken on behalf of the dead:

Let us help and commemorate them. If Job's sons were purified by their father's sacrifice, why would we doubt that our offerings for the dead bring them some consolation? Let us not hesitate to help those who have died and to offer our prayers for them (St. John Chrysostom, *Hom. in 1 Cor.* 41, 5: PG 61, 361; cf. *Job* 1:5).

Can the Holy Souls help us?

Some of the Church's greatest saints have explained that, although the Holy Souls in Purgatory cannot pray for themselves, they can intercede for the living. Saint Alphonsus stated:

They are unable to pray or merit anything for themselves, yet, when they pray for others, they are heard by God.

Saint John Vianney, the Curé d' Ars, wrote:

If one knew what we may obtain from God by the intercession of the Poor Souls, they would not be so much abandoned. Let us pray a great deal for them; they will pray for us.

The Church teaches:

We believe that the multitude of those gathered around Jesus and Mary in Paradise forms the Church of heaven, where in eternal blessedness they see God as he is and where they are also, to various degrees, associated with the holy angels in the divine governance exercised by Christ in glory, by interceding for us and helping our weakness by their fraternal concern (Paul VI, *Credo of the People of God*, 29).

Chapter 2
SCRIPTURES

When we discuss theological concepts such as Purgatory, it's important for Catholics to understand that not every truth we believe is explicitly stated in the Scriptures. Non-Catholics will often point out that the word "Purgatory" doesn't appear anywhere in the Scriptures, and that is certainly true. However, a number of other important Christian teachings are not explicitly stated in the Scriptures, yet both Catholics and other Christians hold them to be true. One of the most obvious examples is the fundamental Christian doctrine of the Trinity. Nowhere in the Scriptures is the word "Trinity" used, and nowhere do we find an explicit definition of the Trinity in all of the New Testament.

We do, however, have in the writings of St. Paul the command, "So then, brethren, stand firm and hold to the traditions which you were taught by us, either by word of mouth or by letter" (2 Thess 2:15). And the reality that truth has been handed on to us by word of mouth — by oral tradition — is foundational to our understanding of the transmission of the Christian faith. After all, the Bible as we have it today did not even get formalized into a single codex until the Councils of Hippo (393) and Carthage (397). So our faith rests in part on almost 400 years of oral tradition.

But Scripture does give us some foundational teaching about Purgatory and the spiritual realities that make it necessary.

Isaiah and Purgatory

When we talk about the biblical evidence for the Catholic theology of Purgatory, I think a good place to begin is with the Prophet Isaiah. Nearly every Christian is at least somewhat familiar with this great prophet of the Old Testament, and Isaiah's reference to being purged of his wretchedness to be prepared for something divine is a good starting point for understanding Purgatory.

Isaiah literally quakes in his boots when he is called by the
Lord to be His prophet:

> Then I said, "Woe is me, I am doomed! For I am a
> man of unclean lips, living among a people of unclean
> lips, and my eyes have seen the King, the Lord of
> hosts!" Then one of the seraphim flew to me, holding
> an ember which he had taken with tongs from the
> altar. He touched my mouth with it. "See," he said,
> "now that this has touched your lips, your wickedness
> is removed, your sin purged" (Is 6:5-7).

Now, one of the central reasons Isaiah is important to us
as Catholics is because of his prophecies about the Suffering
Servant of God, prophecies that we recognize as speaking about
Jesus Christ, by whose stripes we are healed of our iniquities.
(See especially chapters 49-53.) Given Isaiah's prophetic mission
to reveal the future sufferings of the Savior, he was probably a
holy man, or at least a humble man, open to the will of the Lord.
It's telling that even he, a great prophet, recognized his need
to be purged of his sinfulness before serving the Lord. Indeed,
not just the prophet, but the Chosen People needed purification.
Isaiah dramatically describes Israel's need for just such cleansing:
"When the Lord washes away the filth of the daughters of Zion,
and purges Jerusalem's blood from her midst with a blast of judgment, a searing blast" (Is 4:4).

It's fascinating that St. Francis de Sales, the great Catholic
apologist of the 16th century, said this verse from Isaiah can be
interpreted as referring to Purgatory, citing a masterwork by St.
Augustine of Hippo: "This purgation made in the spirit of judgment and of burning is understood of Purgatory by St. Augustine,
in the 20th Book of *The City of God*, ch. 25. And in fact this
interpretation is favored by the words preceding, in which mention is made of the salvation of men, and also by the end of the
chapter, where the repose of the blessed is spoken of; wherefore
that which is said — 'the Lord shall wash away the filth' — is
to be understood of the purgation necessary for this salvation.
And since it is said that this purgation is to be made in the spirit
of heat and of burning, it cannot well be understood save of

Purgatory and its fire" (*The Catholic Controversy*, tr. Henry B. Mackey, OSB, TAN Books, 1989).

But there's more. In Isaiah, we also hear about the necessity of perfect holiness before coming into the presence of the Lord. Just before his calling as a prophet, for example, Isaiah describes his awesome vision of the Lord God "seated on a high and lofty throne," while the angels in his presence constantly cry out, "Holy, holy, holy is the Lord of Hosts!" (Is 6:1-3). That is why Isaiah cries out, "Woe is me, I am doomed!" (Is 6:5).

Like Isaiah, then, we must all undergo a conscious and voluntary purging before approaching the All-Holy God. Especially as we pass from this life into eternity, we will probably still need purgation, so that we might become perfectly holy as God is holy. In Scripture, the necessity of absolute holiness in order to enter Heaven is very clear. Hebrews 12:14 refers to "that holiness without which no one will see the Lord," and Revelation 21:27 declares that "nothing unclean shall enter [there]." On this, Protestants and Catholics are in total agreement. The fundamental disagreement on the subject between Catholics and Protestants is how long this purification after death may take. Certainly, it cannot logically be denied as a *possibility* that this purging might involve a duration of time or a process of some sort, instead of being instantaneous at the moment of death.

New Testament evidence on Purgatory

Now, turning to the New Testament, let's see if there are also certain offenses that indicate the existence of Purgatory. Consider Matthew 5:22: "But I say to you that everyone who is angry with his brother shall be liable to judgment; whoever insults his brother shall be liable to the council, and whoever says, 'You fool!' shall be liable to the hell of fire." And in Matthew 5:25-26, Jesus says: "Make friends quickly with your accuser, while you are going with him to court, lest your accuser hand you over to the judge, and the judge to the guard, and you be put in prison; truly, I say to you, you will never get out till you have paid the last penny."

Referring to Matthew 5:22, St. Francis de Sales points out in *The Catholic Controversy* that "it is only the third sort of offense ["whoever says 'you fool'"] which is punished by hell; therefore, in the judgment of God, there are other pains after this life that are not eternal or infernal — these are the pains of Purgatory." Though the sacred text says that the pains in question will be suffered in this world, St. Augustine and the other Church Fathers understood that this Scripture can also apply to the next world, for "may it not be that a man should die on the first or the second offense which is spoken of here? And when will such a one pay the penalty due to his offense?" So St. Francis concludes, as the Church Fathers did, that we should say that "there is a place where [souls] will be purified, and then they will go to heaven above."

The Rich Man and Lazarus

Next, we'll examine the well-known parable about the Rich Man and Lazarus. This is a parable that comes from Christ, and who would know better about eternal realities than our Merciful Savior?

I have always felt that this story, taken from the Gospel of Luke, gives us one of the best pieces of evidence for Purgatory. Let's read it attentively:

> There was a rich man who dressed in purple garments and fine linen and dined sumptuously each day. And lying at his door was a poor man named Lazarus, covered with sores, who would gladly have eaten his fill of the scraps that fell from the rich man's table. Dogs even used to come and lick his sores. When the poor man died, he was carried away by angels to the bosom of Abraham. The rich man also died and was buried, and from the netherworld, where he was in torment, he raised his eyes and saw Abraham far off and Lazarus at his side. And he cried out, "Father Abraham, have pity on me. Send Lazarus to dip the tip of his finger in water and cool my tongue, for I am suffering torment in these flames." Abraham replied, "My child, remember that you received what was good during your lifetime while Lazarus likewise received what was

bad; but now he is comforted here, whereas you are tormented. Moreover, between us and you a great chasm is established to prevent anyone from crossing who might wish to go from our side to yours or from your side to ours." He said, "Then I beg you, Father, send him to my father's house, for I have five brothers, so that he may warn them, lest they too come to this place of torment." But Abraham replied, "They have Moses and the prophets. Let them listen to them." He said, "Oh no, Father Abraham, but if someone from the dead goes to them, they will repent." Then Abraham said, "If they will not listen to Moses and the prophets, neither will they be persuaded if someone should rise from the dead" (Lk 16:19-31).

Basically, what we have in this parable is that a rich man and a poor man die. The rich man goes to a place of infernal fiery torment, while the poor man Lazarus rests quietly with Abraham. There is a huge abyss that one can't cross over between where the rich man suffers in flames and where Lazarus enjoys a place of rest. This place of rest was where the souls of the saints of the Old Testament awaited the arrival of Jesus.

Sometimes people ask, "What was this place of rest?" Well, it was clearly not Heaven, because Christ is the one who is telling the parable.

You see, when Adam and Eve sinned, the gates of paradise were closed. They are not reopened until Christ dies, descends into Sheol, preaches to the dead, and leads the righteous into Heaven. The place of rest in the parable must have been an intermediate place between Heaven and hell, which the Jews referred to as "Sheol." Sheol was not quite the same as Purgatory because both the righteous and unrighteous would go to Sheol, but it was very close in meaning.

The word "Sheol" is used dozens of times in the Bible. For example, in 2 Samuel 22:5-6, we read: "For the waves of death encompassed me, the torrents of perdition assailed me; the cords of Sheol entangled me, the snares of death confronted me." And in Psalm 86:13, we hear of a soul's deliverance from Sheol:

"Great is thy steadfast love toward me. Thou hast delivered my soul from the depths of Sheol."

In the New Testament, we find a reference to this interme-diate state where Jesus goes to preach after He dies; in 1 Peter 3:19-20, we hear of the place to "which [Jesus] went and preached to the spirits in prison, who formerly did not obey, when God's patience waited in the days of Noah, during the building of the ark, in which a few, that is, eight persons, were saved through water." This place that Christ visited and then departed from is clearly neither hell nor Heaven. After all, Christ did not preach to the damned, and He departed from that place to bring the Old Testament saints into Heaven. As Catholic commentator George Leo Haydock writes:

> "These spirits in prison, to whom Christ went to preach after His death, were not in Heaven, nor in the hell of the damned; because Heaven is no prison, and Christ did not go preach to the damned. ... In this prison, souls would not be detained unless they were indebted to divine justice, nor would salvation be preached to them unless they were in a state that was capable of receiving salvation" (*Haydock's Catholic Family Bible and Commentary,* New York: 1859; rep. Monrovia, CA: Catholic Treasures, 1991).

St. Paul and 'baptism for the dead'

Finally, we'll focus on St. Paul, especially the idea of the baptism for the dead.

In 1 Corinthians 15:29, St. Paul writes, "Otherwise, what do people mean by being baptized on behalf of the dead? If the dead are not raised at all, why are people baptized on their behalf?"

Saint Paul's passage on the baptism for the dead is one of the often terribly misinterpreted passages of Sacred Scripture. This "baptism" is the kind that Jesus is talking about when the mother of the sons of Zebedee comes to Him and says, "Com-mand that these two sons of mine may sit, one at Your right hand and one at Your left, in Your kingdom." And He says to them,

"You do not know what you are asking. Are you able to drink the cup that I am to drink?" (Mt 20:21-22). He is talking about His suffering, His Passion, His scourging, His crown of thorns, His being nailed to the Cross, and then finally His death. "Are you able to drink the cup that I am to drink?" Can the sons of Zebedee accept the baptism with which Jesus will be baptized?

Now, Jesus had already been baptized in the Jordan by John the Baptist, so this baptism is a different baptism. This is a baptism of prayer. It is an offering of suffrages for the sake of others. This baptism that Jesus receives is a baptism of purification and suffering for our sanctification.

This is what St. Francis de Sales had to say about St. Paul's notion of baptism for the dead:

> The passage properly understood evidently shows that it was the custom of the primitive Church to watch, pray, [and] fast for the souls of the departed. For, firstly, in the Scriptures to be baptized is often taken for afflictions and penances; as in [Luke 12:50] ... and [Mark 10:38-39] ... in which places our Lord calls pains and afflictions baptism [see also Mt 3:11; 20:22-3; Lk 3:16]. This then is the sense of that Scripture: if the dead rise not again, what is the use of mortifying and afflicting one's self, of praying and fasting for the dead? And indeed this sentence of St. Paul resembles that of [2 Maccabees 12:44] ... 'It is superfluous and vain to pray for the dead if the dead rise not again.'... Now it was not for those in Paradise, who had no need of it, nor for those in hell, who could get no benefit from it; it was, then, for those in Purgatory (*Catholic Controversy*).

Saint Paul certainly doesn't condemn the practice, whatever it is (his question being merely rhetorical). Given these facts, and the striking resemblance to 2 Maccabees 12:44, the traditional Catholic interpretation seems the most plausible. You can bring Maccabees into the discussion of Purgatory and Scripture because Maccabees is part of the Catholic Bible, but you can't discuss Maccabees when you are talking to Protestants, who reject it as an apocryphal writing. And what Protestants usually mean is that it was not written in the language necessary for it to be accepted as divinely inspired. If it's the Old Testament, it needs to be written in Hebrew, and Maccabees wasn't written in Hebrew. Catholics have always accepted it; it was recognized as canonical at the Council of Hippo in 393.

Now I'd like to share with you three passages from the New Testament, which refer to three levels of reality. The first is Philippians 2:10-11: "That at the name of Jesus every knee should bow, in heaven and on earth and under the earth, and every tongue confess that Jesus Christ is Lord, to the glory of God the Father." Similarly, in Revelation 5:3, we read, "And no one in heaven or on earth or under the earth was able to open the scroll or to look into it." And further, Revelation 5:13: "And I heard every creature in heaven and on earth and under the earth and in the sea, and all therein, saying, 'To him who sits upon the throne and to the Lamb be blessing and honor and glory and might for ever and ever!'"

Obviously, two levels of this three-tiered reality (all those "in Heaven" and "on earth") refer to the Church Triumphant and the Church Militant. But what about those who are referred to as "under the earth"? The reference is certainly not to those in hell. They would not be praising God. But who else would be praising God? By the process of elimination, it must be referring to the Church Suffering in Purgatory.

Some Protestant commentators readily admit that "under the earth" is a reference to those in Sheol or hades. Most Protestants would regard hades in this instance (after Christ's death) as simply the holding tank for those ultimately destined for hell, since the elect would have been taken to Heaven by Christ. But this leads straight back to an exegetical problem of God neither desiring nor accepting such praise from even the obstinate sinner, let alone the damned. If it is conceded that righteous men praise God from "under the earth," the standard Protestant position that all the saved go straight to Heaven at death crumbles.

In 1 Corinthians 3:13-15, St. Paul writes:

> Each man's work will become manifest; for the Day
> will disclose it, because it will be revealed with fire, and

the fire will test what sort of work each one has done. If the work which any man has built on the foundation survives, he will receive a reward. If any man's work is burned up, he will suffer loss, though he himself will be saved, but only as through fire.

In these passages, St. Paul is talking about being tested by fire after death. And clearly he is saying there is another level between Heaven and hell. The place of being tested by fire can't be Heaven, and it can't be hell because no one can be saved there.

Some have suggested that the fire of Purgatory might actually be related to the fire of God's love. We talk about the burning Heart of Jesus, aflame with His love of humanity. We talk about the Immaculate Heart of Mary, consumed with flames of love. Those flames of love are also the zeal of the Holy Spirit that has been placed in the human person. Now, if in fact a Christian has within himself or herself the zeal of the Holy Spirit and is inflamed with the love of God, they might actually feel a certain degree of pain, which St. Paul refers to when he says, "For the desires of the flesh are against the Spirit, and the desires of the Spirit are against the flesh; for these are opposed to each other, to prevent you from doing what you would" (Gal 5:17). As Catholics, we might say that the same torment continues into Purgatory.

These Scriptures are an important foundation for our Catholic understanding of praying for the dead.

Chapter 3

THE EARLY CHURCH FATHERS AND THE HOLY SOULS

Every now and then, people ask about the origins of the Catholic practice of praying for the dead. I remind them that it really begins in seed form in the Scriptures, which we addressed in the last chapter.

But beyond simply pointing out certain passages in Scripture, we have to keep in mind that as Catholics, we don't consider biblical teaching in a vacuum. Rather, guided by the Magisterium (or teaching authority) of the pope and bishops, we consider the Scriptures in light of the Tradition of the Church. And one of the longstanding practices that make up our Catholic Tradition has always been to pray for the souls of the recently departed.

In fact, I was chatting with Fr. John Larson, MIC, about the early Church Fathers and Purgatory when he pointed out, "The practice of prayer for the dead is found very early on in Christian writings, long before the New Testament was codified in the fourth century."

We can find at least one implicit reference as early as the second century: See *The Martyrdom of Polycarp* (A.D. 156), in which St. Polycarp, the 86-year-old bishop of Smyrna, prayed before his arrest for "all those he had ever known" — many of whom must have been dead by that time.

One example that Fr. John likes to mention from the third century is the *Martyrdom of Perpetua and Felicity* (A.D. 202). It includes a clear account of St. Perpetua's prayer for her 7-year-old brother who had died, visions of his suffering in Purgatory, and then his blessed and joyful release:

> I saw Dinocrates coming out of a very dark place, in which I beheld also many other persons. His complexion was very pale, his face covered with perspiration;

his lips seemed parched with a burning fever; he still retained in his cheek the ulcer of which he died, at the age of seven years. ... Therefore, I prayed for him, with many tears, both night and day, asking our Lord to grant me my request. ... I was favored with another vision: I beheld the place, which was so dark and cheerless when I saw it the first time, now charming and filled with light. Dinocrates himself appeared clean, well clad, his countenance full of joy; on his cheek, instead of the frightful cancer, I saw merely a scar. ... When I awoke, I became at once satisfied that he was now free from his pain.

Also, the early Church author Tertullian, writing around A.D. 211, mentions, "We offer sacrifices for the dead on their birthday anniversaries" (*The Crown*, 3:3). This is a reference to the day they died — the day they were born into eternal life. Clearly, the early Church recognized a need for suffrages for the faithful departed.

He also mentions in another text a woman praying for the soul of her husband and asking that he may find rest. Then she offers suffrages on the anniversary of his death. "She prays for his soul, and requests refreshment for him meanwhile, and fellowship (with him) in the first resurrection; and she offers sacrifices on the anniversary of his falling asleep," writes Tertullian (*On Monogamy*, 10:1–2).

Of course, the most powerful sacrifice we can offer for the Holy Souls is that of the Mass.

"We can also look to Origen who, in a homily on Jeremiah given around A.D. 244, points out that 'if a man departs this life with lighter faults, he is condemned to fire which burns away the lighter materials, and prepares the soul for the kingdom of God, where nothing defiled may enter,'" Fr. John tells us.

And in A.D. 253, St. Cyprian wrote to his brother Antonianus:

It is one thing to stand for pardon, another thing to attain to glory. ... It is one thing, tortured by long suffering for sins, to be cleansed and long purged by fire; another to have purged all sins by suffering. It is one thing, in fine, to be in suspense till the sentence of God at the day of judgment; another to be at once crowned by the Lord (*Letters*, 51[55]:20).

We continue to find references to Purgatory in the mid-fourth century, as St. Cyril of Jerusalem, writing about the liturgy, mentions prayer for the dead:

Then we make mention also of those who have already fallen asleep: first, the patriarchs, prophets, apostles, and martyrs, that through their prayers and supplications God would receive our petition; next, we make mention also of the holy fathers and bishops who have already fallen asleep, and, to put it simply, of all among us who have already fallen asleep. For we believe that it will be of very great benefit to the souls of those for whom the petition is carried up, while this holy and most solemn sacrifice is laid out (*Catechetical Lectures*, 23:5:9).

"The prayer for the dead during the Holy Mass is quite ancient, and the above passage shows this practice was well accepted in both East and West," Fr. John points out.

In A.D. 392, St. John Chrysostom wrote:

Let us help and commemorate them. If Job's sons were purified by their father's sacrifice (see Job 1:5), why would we doubt that our offerings for the dead bring them some consolation? Let us not hesitate to help those who have died and to offer our prayers for them (*Homilies on First Corinthians*, 41:5).

In the fifth century, the great Church Father St. Augustine wrote repeatedly of the doctrine of Purgatory and intercession for the dead. Indeed, 40 passages in his books make mention of praying for the dead. Consider this one, in which Augustine shares well-developed teaching on prayer for the dead, emphasizing it as a work of mercy:

But by the prayers of the holy Church, and by the salvific sacrifice, and by the alms which are given for their spirits, there is no doubt that the dead are aided, that the Lord might deal more mercifully with them than their sins would deserve. The whole Church observes this practice which was handed down by the Fathers: that it prays for those who have died in the communion of the Body and Blood of Christ, when they are commemorated in their own place in the sacrifice itself; and the sacrifice is offered also in memory of them, on their behalf. If, then, works of mercy are celebrated for the sake of those who are being remembered, who would hesitate to recommend them, on whose behalf prayers to God are not offered in vain? It is not at all to be doubted that such prayers are of profit to the dead; but for such of them as lived before their death in a way that makes it possible for these things to be useful to them after death (*Sermons*, 172:2).

By the sixth century, St. Caesarius of Arles not only articulates what Purgatory is, but the manner in which God uses it to purify us:

If we neither return thanks to God in tribulation, nor redeem sins with good works, we shall stay in the purgatorial fire until the above-named small sins be consumed like wood, hay and stubble ... But someone says: I don't mind how long I stay there if at length I shall arrive at eternal life. Let no one say this, dearest brethren, because that Purgatory fire shall be severer than any punishment that can be either thought of, or seen, or felt in this world. How can anyone know whether he is about to pass through that fire for days and months or perhaps even for years? (*Sermons*, 179 (104):2).

Father John concludes, "And finally, Pope St. Gregory the Great, who reigned from A.D. 590-604, said, 'It must be believed that there is a purgatorial fire for some light faults before judgment ... but we must believe that this can only happen in the case of small and very small sins'" (*Dialogues*, 4:39).

We can see, then, that our Tradition of praying for the souls in Purgatory has been a part of Catholic belief from the earliest times in the life of the Church. May this knowledge inspire us to see the sure foundation for our devotion to the Holy Souls. And let us ask these early Church Fathers and saints to join us in interceding for the suffering souls, especially those most forgotten.

Chapter 4

CHURCH COUNCILS ON PURGATORY

I would like to share a little history lesson by
Fr. John Larson, MIC:

The specific idea of purification after death is not codified in the teaching of the Church until the Middle Ages. Some argue that this shows that Purgatory was invented. It should be noted, however, that all liturgies by the end of the fourth century clearly include prayers for the dead. Up to the time of the Reformation, the idea of prayer for the dead was firmly established in all corners of the Christian world. The question that remained, and still is a source of contention between Catholic and Orthodox, is what sort of state the dead might be in who were not yet in Heaven. In general, Orthodox theology has rejected the specific concept of Purgatory, but not necessarily the idea that there is purification after this life. Since the theology had not been worked out at the time of the schism between East and West, the debates over the nature of the state of the dead who are not in Heaven or hell is still debated in the East, and no pronouncements have been made.

In the West, however, we have the declaration of the Second Council of Lyons in 1274, which states:

> If those who are truly repentant die in charity before they have done sufficient penance for their sins of omission and commission, their souls are cleansed after death in purgatorial or cleansing punishments ... The suffrages of the faithful on earth can be of great help in relieving these punishments, as, for instance, the Sacrifice of the Mass, prayers, almsgiving, and other religious deeds which, in the manner of the Church, the faithful are accustomed to offer for others of the faithful (*The Church Teaches: Documents of the Church in English Translation,* Herder, 1955, pp. 348-349).

There are further declarations, such as that of Benedict XII, who in his constitution *Benedictus Deus*, issued in 1336, stated:

> According to the general disposition of God, the souls of all the saints who departed from this world before the passion of our Lord Jesus Christ and also of the holy apostles, martyrs, confessors, virgins and other faithful who died after receiving the holy baptism of Christ — provided they were not in need of any purification when they died, or will not be in need of any when they die in the future, or else, if they then needed or will need some purification, after they have been purified after death ... immediately (*mox*) after death and, in the case of those in need of purification, after the purification mentioned above, since the ascension of our Lord and Savior Jesus Christ into heaven, already before they take up their bodies again and before the general judgment, have been, are and will be with Christ in heaven, in the heavenly kingdom and paradise, joined to the company of the holy angels.

As the doctrine of Purgatory was attacked during the time of the Reformation, Pope Leo X in 1520 condemned the following propositions of Martin Luther: "Purgatory cannot be proved from the Sacred Scripture which is the Canon. The souls in purgatory are not sure about their salvation, at least not all of them."

The Council of Trent first defined Purgatory in a negative way, stating that to deny it is heresy. Shortly before the closing sessions of the council, the following statements were made in a decree on Purgatory:

> The Catholic Church, by the teaching of the Holy Spirit, in accordance with Sacred Scripture and the ancient tradition of the Fathers, has taught in the holy councils, and most recently in this ecumenical council, that there is a purgatory, and that the souls detained there are helped by the prayers of the faithful, and especially by the acceptable Sacrifice of the Altar. Therefore, this holy council commands the bishops to be diligently on guard that the true doctrine about

purgatory, the doctrine handed down from the holy Fathers and the sacred councils, be preached everywhere, and that Christians be instructed in it, believe it, and adhere to it (*The Church Teaches,* p. 352).

I have occasionally heard of diaconal or seminary training that declared that the Catholic Church no longer believes in Purgatory. Let us be clear: The Catholic Church will never stop believing in Purgatory until the end of the world. Denial of the teaching on Purgatory probably still happens in some places, but rest assured, the teaching is clearly outlined in magisterial documents from the Second Vatican Council. The Vatican II document *Lumen Gentium* mentions briefly the state of purification:

> Until the Lord shall come in his majesty, and all the angels with him (see Mt 25:31) and death being destroyed, all things are subject to him (see 1 Cor 15:26-27), some of his disciples are exiles on earth, *some having died are purified,* and others are in glory beholding "clearly God himself triune and one, as he is"; but all in various ways and degrees are in communion in the same charity of God and neighbor and all sing the same hymn of glory to our God (*LG*, 49).

Also, the second edition of the *Catechism* (United States Conference of Catholic Bishops, 2000) has this glossary entry:

> A state of final purification after death and before entrance into heaven for those who died in God's friendship, but were only imperfectly purified; a final cleansing of human imperfection before one is able to enter the joy of heaven.

Although some obfuscation of the teaching occurred in the chaos after Vatican II, along with many basic teachings, there is no need to be concerned about the official teachings. The age-old tradition of praying for the dead is in every liturgy — in the Eucharistic prayers themselves. The doctrine is really inescapable if one examines the history of the Church.

Chapter 5

CAN SAINTS PRAY FOR THE HOLY SOULS?

I was once asked by a Sodality member if the saints in Heaven pray for the souls in Purgatory as we do here on earth. While I was pondering this question, I found an interesting article from the Zenit online news service. It was by a Legionary of Christ priest, Fr. Edward McNamara, professor of liturgy at the Regina Apostolorum Pontifical Athenaeum in Rome, and he was fielding the very same question. I thought we could explore his answer together:

> The question is more theological than liturgical and very speculative theology at that, but is also very intriguing. The crux of the question revolves around the way that the saints in heaven can know the realities that occur on earth and in purgatory.
>
> In general, most theologians hold that once a person enters into the realm of the beatific vision, they do not have universal access to our thoughts or to earthly reality.
>
> Any knowledge they gain is received directly from God, and God most certainly makes them aware of requests for their intercession in a way that we can only imagine but never fully grasp while remaining here below.
>
> Therefore I believe we can confidently affirm that the saints intercede for the souls in purgatory in those cases when someone on earth requests that saint's intercession for a particular soul (Zenit.org, "Saints' Prayers for Souls in Purgatory," April 1, 2008).

So, according to Fr. McNamara, the key to getting a saint to intercede for a departed soul is "when someone on earth requests that saint's intercession for a particular soul." This is a very important point. Here is where our duty as the Church Militant comes in. We have a duty not only to pray for the Holy Souls, the Church Suffering, and for their release since they are unable to pray for themselves, but we also have a duty to ask the saints, the Church Triumphant, to intercede for the Holy Souls. This is part of our role in the Communion of Saints.

Once we've asked a saint to intercede for a departed soul, what exactly can that saint do for the soul?

Saint Thomas Aquinas explains that the saints do, indeed, have the power to intercede, but that they cannot do things to help gain satisfaction for the souls ("offer suffrages") as we, the Church Militant, can. If they had the ability to offer suffrages, they could easily empty Purgatory, but in Heaven, that's not an option (see the Supplement to the *Summa Theologiae*, question 72, article 3).

Here, it's helpful to clarify what is meant by offering suffrages:

> The prayers prescribed or promised for specific intentions. More particularly, suffrages are the Masses, prayers, or acts of piety offered for the repose of the souls of the faithful departed (Catholic Dictionary at CatholicCulture.org).

Following this line of thought, it's clear that while the saints' prayers for the Holy Souls still have a particular power, we are able to do something here on earth that they are not able to do in Heaven. We can offer suffrages for the Holy Souls in Purgatory to help lessen their suffering and speed them on their way home to Heaven.

It should be noted that among the saints, the Blessed Virgin Mary has by far the greatest ability to intercede on behalf of the Holy Souls. Why? She is Mother of the Church Suffering. Saint Thomas Aquinas explains that Our Lady's role in interceding for the Church is unique, because she was involved in the meriting of all graces as the associate with the Redeemer in His work of redemption at the Cross. Her mediation is universal, and thus she has a special ability to help the souls in Purgatory.

Saint Faustina refers to Our Lady comforting the souls in Purgatory in her *Diary*:

> I saw Our Lady visiting the souls in Purgatory. The souls call her "The Star of the Sea." She brings them refreshment (*Diary of Saint Maria Faustina Kowalska*, 20).

Turning back to Fr. McNamara's article, he says further of the saints' intercession for the Holy Souls:

> The Church itself invokes the saints in this way, albeit in a universal manner, during the rite of final commendation at the graveside at the prayer of the faithful:
>
> > **V.** Saints of God come to his/her aid! Come to meet him/her angels of the Lord!
> >
> > **R.** Receive his/her soul and present him/her to God the Most High.

If the Church proposes a prayer to implore that the saints come to the aid of the dead, then it clearly believes this aid is possible.

From a theological standpoint it is very difficult to be able to affirm that saints intercede, on their own initiative, so to speak, for the souls in purgatory without some form of earthly intercession.

It does not mean it does not happen; it is just that we have no way of knowing.

It is also possible that in a general way the saint's participation in the heavenly liturgy continually glorifying God is also of benefit to the souls in purgatory, but once more we are ignorant of the precise manner in which this might come about.

As the poet Thomas Grey said: "Where ignorance is bliss, 'Tis folly to be wise."

If we were sure that the saints of heaven were independently praying for the souls in purgatory, perhaps many would defer the act of spiritual charity of praying for the deceased to the saint's powerful intercession.

The blessing of ignorance obliges us to continue exercising this intercession on our own, in the hope that others will do likewise for us when we are gone.

As we "continue exercising this intercession on our own" for the Holy Souls, we must remember that those souls are the most poor. They are fully dependent on us. One of the points that Sodality members mention to me most often is that they want to be remembered in prayers when they are gone. Nobody wants to be forgotten when they are unable to help themselves.

From Fr. McNamara's answer, it seems very likely that the saints can intercede for our deceased loved ones if we do our part by bringing their souls to the attention of the saints. And Mary's mediation is unique and universal as Mother of the Church Suffering. Beyond this, the intercession the saints can exercise for the Holy Souls remains a mystery. Further, we have our own vital role to play for the Holy Souls in offering our suffrages (see definition above) for their release from Purgatory.

So, remind the saints you know — especially Our Lady — to pray for particular souls, and then do your part by offering suffrages for those souls. After all, you're part of the family known as the Communion of Saints. You have a role to play.

Chapter 6

SAINT JOHN PAUL II AND THE HOLY SOULS

I would like Fr. John Larson, MIC, to share with you some of St. John Paul II's 1999 teachings on how we understand Purgatory:

Every trace of attachment to evil must be eliminated, every imperfection of the soul corrected. Purification must be complete, and indeed this is precisely what is meant by the Church's teaching on Purgatory. The term does not indicate a place, but a condition of existence. Those who, after death, exist in a state of purification, are already in the love of Christ who removes from them the remnants of imperfection (see Ecumenical Council of Florence, *Decretum pro Graecis*: DS 1304; Ecumenical Council of Trent, *Decretum de iustificatione:* DS 1580; *Decretum de purgatorio*: DS 1820) — St. John Paul II, General Audience, August 4, 1999.

Pope John Paul II made some waves in the Church when he stated in this Wednesday audience of August 4, 1999, that the term "Purgatory" does not "indicate a place, but a condition of existence." Often, Purgatory is thought of as a place, and described as such even by saints. Was he offering a new way of looking at Purgatory?

Not really. Purgatory has never been defined by the Church as a particular place, although there are private revelations that seem to show Purgatory as a place. Some private revelations involving visits to Purgatory describe a number of levels of Purgatory, often with the highest being a field of flowers — a sort of "waiting area" for Heaven. The most important thing, which the Church teaches emphatically, is that this purifying condition of souls exists.

Thus, St. John Paul II was wise in not focusing on Purgatory as a place, but a condition of existence. This is the solid teaching of the early Church. Why must Purgatory exist? The justice of God is many faceted, but it is also important to remember that the mercy of God is infinite.

Purgatory is essentially a process of purification. We can get caught up in the idea of "place," but first and foremost, Purgatory is a process that in some way involves purification from our sins.

Pope John Paul II describes our need for this kind of purification:

> For those who find themselves in a condition of being open to God, but still imperfectly, the journey towards full beatitude requires a purification, which the faith of the Church illustrates in the doctrine of "Purgatory" (see *Catechism*, 1030-1032).

A biblical basis for this teaching on the need for purification is found in one of the Scripture references in the *Catechism* passage St. John Paul II cites: "But if someone's work is burned up, that one will suffer loss; the person will be saved, but only as through a fire" (1 Cor 3:15). Here we have the Apostle Paul's mention of the need for spiritual cleansing.

Of course, Purgatory is not directly referred to in this passage. Nevertheless, we can grasp certain elements that help us to understand the meaning of this doctrine, even if it is not formally described anywhere in Sacred Scripture. These elements substantiate the belief that we cannot approach God without undergoing some kind of purification.

Remember the key words about "being open to God, but still imperfectly" in our earlier quote from Pope John Paul II's teaching? What we're after in this life and the next is perfection in order to approach God because He is perfect. According to Old Testament religious law, whatever is destined for God must be perfect. Physical integrity is even specifically required for what comes into contact with God at the sacrificial level in the Temple (such as, for example, sacrificial animals [see Lv 22:22]), or at the institutional level (as in the case of priests or ministers of worship [see Lv 21:17-23]). Total dedication to the God of the Covenant, along the lines of the great teachings found in Deuteronomy (see 6:5), which must correspond to this physical integrity, is required of individuals and society as a whole (see 1 Kgs 8:61). It's a matter of loving God with all our being, with purity of heart, and the witness of deeds.

Such integrity is necessary for entering into perfect and complete communion with God. Those who do not possess this complete integrity after death, and yet are headed to Heaven, must undergo purification, as our earlier passage from St. Paul attests in describing a cleansing fire for certain souls.

A comforting truth that St. John Paul II points out in his catechesis is that these souls "are already in the love of Christ who removes from them the remnants of imperfection." They died in the state of grace and are guaranteed to reach Heaven.

Pope John Paul II stressed the need to pray for the souls in Purgatory at several points throughout his papacy. In a letter sent to the Minim Sisters of Our Lady of Suffrage as they held their general chapter in Rome, dated Sept 2, 2002, the Pope emphasized their call to pray for the Holy Souls: "Concern for prayer for the souls of Purgatory is your specific charism, Reverend Mother and dear sisters, which impels you to pray constantly for those who have gone before us. The same charismatic intuition is a concrete incentive to fill every one of our earthly days with the goods that do not fade or spoil." He stated, "The first and highest form of charity for brothers is the ardent desire for their eternal salvation. Christian love knows no bounds and is removed from the bounds of space and time, allowing us to love those who have already left this earth."

Certainly St. John Paul II — who had lost all of his immediate family members by the time he was a young man — prayed fervently for his family's souls, especially those of his father and mother. Like him, our need to show Christian love extends to those suffering in Purgatory, especially our departed loved ones, and this can be done in a variety of ways. It is possible to do a work of charity for the living and offer it up for the dead, thus showing charity to both the living and the dead at the same time.

Interestingly, Pope John Paul II's 1999 catechesis on Purgatory does not emphasize punishment, but rather focuses on purification, which is what the word "purgation" means. We have to be perfect to enter Heaven, so we must be purified of all imperfections. Let us be mindful of those who are in this condition and ask for the mercy of God to be shown to them.

Let us follow the words of St. John Paul II and "pray constantly for those who have gone before us."

We are called to perform works of mercy. May I suggest you focus on the spiritual work of praying for the Holy Souls?

Chapter 7

POPE BENEDICT XVI AND THE HOLY SOULS

Pope Emeritus Benedict XVI is devoted to the Holy Souls. I would like to share some passages from his encyclical letter of November 30, 2007, *Spe Salvi*, in which he writes about Purgatory:

44. [...] In the parable of the rich man and Lazarus (cf. Lk 16:19-31), Jesus admonishes us through the image of a soul destroyed by arrogance and opulence, who has created an impassable chasm between himself and the poor man; the chasm of being trapped within material pleasures; the chasm of forgetting the other, of incapacity to love, which then becomes a burning and unquenchable thirst. We must note that in this parable Jesus is not referring to the final destiny after the Last Judgement, but is taking up a notion found, *inter alia*, in early Judaism, namely that of an intermediate state between death and resurrection, a state in which the final sentence is yet to be pronounced.

45. This early Jewish idea of an intermediate state includes the view that these souls are not simply in a sort of temporary custody but, as the parable of the rich man illustrates, are already being punished or are experiencing a provisional form of bliss. There is also the idea that this state can involve purification and healing which mature the soul for communion with God. The early Church took up these concepts, and in the Western Church they gradually developed into the doctrine of Purgatory. We do not need to examine here the complex historical paths of this development; it is enough to ask what it actually means. With death, our life-choice becomes definitive — our life stands before the judge. Our choice, which in the course

of an entire life takes on a certain shape, can have a variety of forms. There can be people who have totally destroyed their desire for truth and readiness to love, people for whom everything has become a lie, people who have lived for hatred and have suppressed all love within themselves. This is a terrifying thought, but alarming profiles of this type can be seen in certain figures of our own history. In such people all would be beyond remedy and the destruction of good would be irrevocable: this is what we mean by the word Hell. On the other hand there can be people who are utterly pure, completely permeated by God, and thus fully open to their neighbours—people for whom communion with God even now gives direction to their entire being and whose journey towards God only brings to fulfilment what they already are.

46. Yet we know from experience that neither case is normal in human life. For the great majority of people — we may suppose — there remains in the depths of their being an ultimate interior openness to truth, to love, to God. In the concrete choices of life, however, it is covered over by ever new compromises with evil — much filth covers purity, but the thirst for purity remains and it still constantly re-emerges from all that is base and remains present in the soul. What happens to such individuals when they appear before the Judge? Will all the impurity they have amassed through life suddenly cease to matter? What else might occur? Saint Paul, in his First Letter to the Corinthians, gives us an idea of the differing impact of God's judgement according to each person's particular circumstances. He does this using images which in some way try to express the invisible, without it being possible for us to conceptualize these images — simply because we can neither see into the world beyond death nor do we have any experience of it. Paul begins by saying that Christian life is built upon a common foundation: Jesus Christ. This foundation

endures. If we have stood firm on this foundation and built our life upon it, we know that it cannot be taken away from us even in death. Then Paul continues: "Now if any one builds on the foundation with gold, silver, precious stones, wood, hay, straw — each man's work will become manifest; for the Day will disclose it, because it will be revealed with fire, and the fire will test what sort of work each one has done. If the work which any man has built on the foundation survives, he will receive a reward. If any man's work is burned up, he will suffer loss, though he himself will be saved, but only as through fire" (1 Cor 3:12-15). In this text, it is in any case evident that our salvation can take different forms, that some of what is built may be burned down, that in order to be saved we personally have to pass through "fire" so as to become fully open to receiving God and able to take our place at the table of the eternal marriage-feast.

47. Some recent theologians are of the opinion that the fire which both burns and saves is Christ himself, the Judge and Saviour. The encounter with him is the decisive act of judgement. Before his gaze all falsehood melts away. This encounter with him, as it burns us, transforms and frees us, allowing us to become truly ourselves. All that we build during our lives can prove to be mere straw, pure bluster, and it collapses. Yet in the pain of this encounter, when the impurity and sickness of our lives become evident to us, there lies salvation. His gaze, the touch of his heart heals us through an undeniably painful transformation "as through fire". But it is a blessed pain, in which the holy power of his love sears through us like a flame, enabling us to become totally ourselves and thus totally of God. In this way the interrelation between justice and grace also becomes clear: the way we live our lives is not immaterial, but our defilement does not stain us forever if we have at least continued to reach out towards Christ, towards truth and towards

love. Indeed, it has already been burned away through Christ's Passion. At the moment of judgement we experience and we absorb the overwhelming power of his love over all the evil in the world and in ourselves. The pain of love becomes our salvation and our joy. It is clear that we cannot calculate the "duration" of this transforming burning in terms of the chronological measurements of this world. The transforming "moment" of this encounter eludes earthly time-reckoning — it is the heart's time, it is the time of "passage" to communion with God in the Body of Christ. The judgement of God is hope, both because it is justice and because it is grace. If it were merely grace, making all earthly things cease to matter, God would still owe us an answer to the question about justice — the crucial question that we ask of history and of God. If it were merely justice, in the end it could bring only fear to us all. The incarnation of God in Christ has so closely linked the two together — judgement and grace — that justice is firmly established: we all work out our salvation "with fear and trembling" (Phil 2:12). Nevertheless grace allows us all to hope, and to go trustfully to meet the Judge whom we know as our "advocate," or *parakletos* (cf. 1 Jn 2:1).

48. A further point must be mentioned here, because it is important for the practice of Christian hope. Early Jewish thought includes the idea that one can help the deceased in their intermediate state through prayer (see for example 2 Macc 12:38-45; first century BC). The equivalent practice was readily adopted by Christians and is common to the Eastern and Western Church. The East does not recognize the purifying and expiatory suffering of souls in the after-life, but it does acknowledge various levels of beatitude and of suffering in the intermediate state. The souls of the departed, however, can receive "solace and refresh-ment" through the Eucharist, prayer and almsgiving. The belief that love can reach into the afterlife, that

reciprocal giving and receiving is possible, in which
our affection for one another continues beyond the
limits of death — this has been a fundamental convic-
tion of Christianity throughout the ages and it remains
a source of comfort today. Who would not feel the
need to convey to their departed loved ones a sign of
kindness, a gesture of gratitude or even a request for
pardon? Now a further question arises: if "Purgatory"
is simply purification through fire in the encounter
with the Lord, Judge and Saviour, how can a third
person intervene, even if he or she is particularly close
to the other? When we ask such a question, we should
recall that no man is an island, entire of itself. Our
lives are involved with one another, through innumerable interactions they are linked together. No one
lives alone. No one sins alone. No one is saved alone.
The lives of others continually spill over into mine:
in what I think, say, do and achieve. And conversely,
my life spills over into that of others: for better and
for worse. So my prayer for another is not something
extraneous to that person, something external, not
even after death. In the interconnectedness of Being,
my gratitude to the other — my prayer for him — can
play a small part in his purification. And for that there
is no need to convert earthly time into God's time:
in the communion of souls simple terrestrial time is
superseded. It is never too late to touch the heart of
another, nor is it ever in vain. In this way we further
clarify an important element of the Christian concept
of hope. Our hope is always essentially also hope for
others; only thus is it truly hope for me too. As Christians we should never limit ourselves to asking: how
can I save myself? We should also ask: what can I do in
order that others may be saved and that for them too
the star of hope may rise? Then I will have done my
utmost for my own personal salvation as well.

SECTION 2

PURGATORY
and the
MARIAN CHARISMS

As I wrote in my introduction, part of the Marian Fathers' charism — their special calling from Christ and their Holy Spirit-inspired path to especially serve His Church — is to offer prayer and sacrifice for the Holy Souls in Purgatory. This was one of the main reasons why I joined the Marians, and part of the reason why St. Stanislaus Papczynski founded the Marians in the first place. The rest of the Marian Fathers' charism is to honor and promote the mystery of the Immaculate Conception of the Blessed Virgin Mary and help parish priests where the need is the greatest. In addition to this, the Marians have been given the added apostolate of spreading the message and devotion to the Divine Mercy given to St. Maria Faustina Kowalska, the apostle of Divine Mercy. In the next collection of writings, you will learn how Mary, St. Stanislaus, and St. Faustina are all key players in this important work of mercy: easing the suffering of the Holy Souls in Purgatory.

Chapter 8
ALL ABOUT MARY

How can Mary help?

We find Our Lady's image in the catacombs of St. Priscilla, going back to the second century. Placing Mary's image next to a tomb indicates the desire to place the deceased under her intercession, as well as an appeal to the living to commend to her the souls of the departed.

In the fourth century, both in the Eastern and Western Churches, we see tombstone inscriptions invoking Mary's intercession for the eternal peace of the deceased.

Awareness of Mary's help for the souls of the departed begins to be completely developed in the Middle Ages. Texts of theologians and preachers appear, which attempt to explain the link between Mary and the mystery of Purgatory (her motherly love, queenship, and intercession). We also have more descriptions of visions and apparitions in which Mary is shown among the Holy Souls in Purgatory as a mother, bringing help and consolation.

From the standpoint of official Church teachings, there is at least one thing that points to Mary helping the souls in Purgatory: an ancient prayer of the Mass. It is the collect or opening prayer for a Mass celebrated for deceased relatives, friends, and benefactors, and it is the same in both the extraordinary and ordinary forms of the Latin Rite. The new English translation of this prayer is:

> O God, giver of pardon and loving author of our salvation, grant, we pray you, in your mercy, that through the intercession of Blessed Mary, ever-Virgin, and all your Saints, the members, friends, and benefactors of our community, who have passed from this world, may attain a share in eternal happiness. Through our Lord Jesus Christ, your Son, who lives and reigns with

you in the unity of the Holy Spirit, one God, for ever
and ever (*Roman Missal*, 3rd Edition, p. 1413).

Clearly, the Church believes that the prayers of Our Lady
and the saints can be helpful to the souls in Purgatory.

Mary has the ability to intercede in a special way: In the
Raccolta, a manual of indulgences, we find a prayer to offer as a
request to the sorrowful Virgin Mary:

> Present unto Him (the Eternal Father), together with
> the dolorous Passion of thy dear Son, thine own sighs
> and tears, and all the sorrows thou didst suffer in His
> suffering, in order that, through the merits of the
> same, refreshment may be granted to the souls now
> suffering in the fiery torments of Purgatory" (Prayer
> no. 595 in the 1952 edition).

Her participation at the foot of the cross in the work of
redemption gives her the ability to intercede for the Holy Souls
in a special way. Our Lady is in a special situation because she was
involved in the meriting of all graces as the Redeemer's associate
in the work of redemption. Her mediation is universal, and thus
she has a special ability to help the souls in Purgatory.

Many saints were confident of Our Lady's intercession for
the Holy Souls.

Mary is the 'consolation of the souls in Purgatory': In
the writings of St. Brigid, she tells about hearing Jesus say to His
Mother: "You are My Mother, the Mother of Mercy, and the
consolation of the souls in Purgatory." She also mentions Mary
telling her that as a poor, sick person, bedridden, suffering, and
abandoned, is relieved by words of encouragement and consolation, so are the souls in Purgatory consoled and relieved by only
hearing her name.

Souls are often visited and relieved by Mary: Saint
Bernardine of Siena discusses Purgatory in a similar manner,
explaining "that the pains of Purgatory are called waves, because
they are transitory, unlike the pains of hell, which never end; and
they are called waves of the sea, because they are so bitter. The
clients of Mary, thus suffering, are often visited and relieved by
her" (St. Alphonsus Liguori, *The Glories of Mary*).

Finally, I will quote from an anonymously written article from *The Marian* (a magazine the Marian Fathers in Chicago published in the past) called "The Mother of All the Souls in Purgatory":

> Since Mary, Our Blessed Lady, is so solicitous for the souls suffering in purgatory, we must recommend our faithfully departed friends and relatives to her sincere prayers and intercession. [Let us pray] the Rosary for them. It must be recited often for the souls in purgatory, and it is here that we must develop a zeal for being present at the wakes of friends when the Rosary is recited for their repose. Mary must be asked to take their souls under her special protection, so that they too may be relieved of their sufferings (November 1959, p. 4).

So please remember at Mass and in your prayers to ask the Queen of the Suffering Souls for her intercession. May she bring them consolation and relief, and may she welcome many of them into the glories of Heaven.

Mary's compassion for the Holy Souls

By Fr. Donald Calloway, MIC

I asked Fr. Donald Calloway, MIC, who has completed advanced studies in Mariology, to share about Our Lady and her compassion for the Holy Souls in Purgatory:
I think one of the main reasons for Mary's compassion for the souls in Purgatory is because they are her spiritual children. She is the Mother of the Mystical Body of Christ, and the souls in Purgatory are members of the Mystical Body of Christ — they are the Church Suffering. But even more than that, it's because she is a mother. What mother would not want to take care of her children? So it's not as though Mary ever forgets the Holy Souls in Purgatory, or that she is not going to help them in any way possible. Of course she will, by her prayers and intercession for them. There is never ever anyone left out of her compassion. And

her Son surely must let her know who among the suffering souls is the most forgotten or who among them is the most in need.

As you see in the lives of certain saints, such as St. Faustina, Mary visits the Church Suffering in Purgatory. She takes the graces from the members of the Church Militant, who are offering up their sacrifices, penances, and prayers for the Holy Souls, and distributes those graces from God to the souls in Purgatory.

In my book about Mary in the spiritual life of St. Faustina, *Purest of All Lilies*, I write about Mary being the Mother of Mercy and how St. Faustina expressed her understanding of the Mother of Mercy's intercession for the souls in Purgatory.

During her postulancy (1925-1926), St. Faustina relates that on one occasion she was given the experience of visiting the souls in Purgatory, and while there, she witnessed the merciful intercession of Mary:

> I saw my Guardian Angel, who ordered me to follow him. In a moment I was in a misty place full of fire in which there was a great crowd of suffering souls. They were praying fervently, but to no avail, for themselves; only we can come to their aid. The flames which were burning them did not touch me at all. My Guardian Angel did not leave me for an instant. I asked these souls what their greatest suffering was. They answered in one voice that their greatest torment was longing for God. I saw Our Lady visiting the souls in Purgatory. The souls call her "Star of the Sea." She brings them refreshment. I wanted to talk with them some more, but my Guardian Angel beckoned me to leave. … Since that time, I am in closer communication with the suffering souls (*Diary*, 20).

Saint Faustina understood Mary as the "Star of the Sea," bringing the souls in Purgatory refreshment, meaning that Mary intercedes for them so that their purification might be quickened. Experiencing this visit to Purgatory at the beginning of her religious life was undoubtedly an encouragement for her constant intercession for the Holy Souls. We also know that the Marian element played an important part in St. Faustina's prayers for the souls in Purgatory, since she noted that she prayed the Rosary in order to aid them (see *Diary*, 314).

Furthermore, on the Solemnity of the Assumption in 1937, Mary told St. Faustina that those who persevere faithfully in her religious community will be spared the fire of Purgatory (see *Diary*, 1244).

So we know Mary brings refreshment to the souls in Purgatory. And she does this often because she's a good mother. She loves her children. She doesn't want to see her children suffering, but she knows it's part of the justice of God that our sins have consequences, so souls have to be purified. She is such a good mother that she wants to help them along, even speeding up the process so that they can enter into Heaven sooner.

As I say in my book *Under the Mantle* (Marian Press, 2013), Mary is like the heart in the Mystical Body of Christ — just as any good mother is the heart of her family. She circulates the life-blood of graces to all the members. It's not just for the members here on earth but also for the members in Purgatory, who are her children as well. That's what a heart does: It pumps the blood, which is the source of life, to all the members of the body. By no means are the souls in Purgatory forgotten: Mary is also the Mediatrix of God's mercy and grace for them.

After reading this, I think you should be incredibly excited. You have the ear of our Mother of Mercy! She is working tirelessly to bring our prayers, our sufferings, and our trials for the Holy Souls in Purgatory to God's mercy seat in Heaven. We should be striving to give her even more prayers and sacrifices that she can use to help those souls. When we undergo difficulty throughout our day — in our family situation, in the workplace, or wherever it may be — when we give all of that to Our Lady, she takes it to her Son, who is Divine Mercy Incarnate. She takes them to her Son on our behalf because we give everything to her. Then she can, as our spiritual mother, intercede before the Holy Trinity, the mercy seat, and help the souls in Purgatory with all of our contributions.

When you are carrying a heavy cross, you basically are giving a spiritual bouquet to Our Lady. She can apply the benefits and merits of your suffering to the souls in Purgatory who are in greatest need, because we share in that spiritual exchange of goods. That's the amazing thing about being members of the Mystical Body of Christ and having such a loving mother who is attentive to the needs of all the members of the body, all of whom are her children.

Our Lady is actually looking for her children, who are members of the Church Militant, to be willing to offer up their sufferings and prayers for the Holy Souls, so that she can distribute those graces and lessen our brothers' and sisters' time in Purgatory.

Marian Consecration and the Holy Souls

By Fr. Michael Gaitley, MIC

I asked Fr. Michael Gaitley, MIC, who wrote the bestseller, 33 Days to Morning Glory: A Do-It-Yourself Retreat In Preparation for Marian Consecration, *to share some of his thoughts about Mary and Purgatory:*

We should all have two main concerns regarding Purgatory: (1) avoiding it and (2) helping souls get out of it. Here, I'd like to propose one of the best (and easiest) ways to avoid Purgatory and to help souls get out of it. It's called Marian consecration.

1. Marian consecration is one of the best ways to avoid Purgatory

Believe it or not, Purgatory is a gift of God's mercy. It allows us to pay for the punishment due to our sins after we die — without going to hell. Even though Purgatory is a gift, Jesus doesn't want us to go there. He wants us to have a "direct flight" to Heaven to be with Him when we die. In other words, He doesn't want us to suffer the uncomfortable layover of Purgatory, which delays our full communion with Him. So, how can we get the direct flight and avoid the layover? I suggest that we consecrate ourselves to Mary.

According to St. Louis de Montfort, total consecration to Jesus through Mary is "the quickest, easiest, surest, and most perfect" way to grow in holiness and to become a saint. In other words, Marian consecration is the quickest, easiest, surest, and most perfect way to avoid Purgatory! It may be our best shot at getting a direct flight to Heaven when we die. All right, so what does Marian consecration mean?

Basically, Marian consecration means to formally entrust ourselves to the care of our spiritual Mother, Mary. In fact, it's simply to do what God Himself did. In Jesus Christ, at the moment of the Incarnation, God entrusted Himself to Mary's care. It's also something that God wants us to do. In fact, Jesus already entrusted us to His Mother. It happened when He was dying on the Cross. He looked down at Mary and John, the Beloved Disciple, and said to Mary, "Woman, behold your son" and to John, "Behold your mother" (Jn 19:26-27).

According to Pope John Paul II, the Beloved Disciple represents all of us, and therefore, on the Cross, Jesus entrusted us all to Mary. The Pope says that we should actively accept Mary's care, and that we should respond to the gift of Mary's spiritual motherhood like John, who took Mary "into his own home." John Paul explains that this welcoming of Mary into our own home means "to bring her into everything that makes up [our] inner life" (*Redemptoris Mater*, 45). It means giving her the merits of our prayers and good works (more on this later), bringing her our hopes and disappointments, joys and sorrows, anxieties and fears.

This encouragement to entrust ourselves to Mary doesn't just come from St. John Paul II. In fact, the Second Vatican Council taught, "Everyone should have a genuine devotion to [Mary] and entrust his life to her motherly care." Why? Because Mary does the best job in helping us become holy and getting us on a "direct flight" to Jesus when we die. As St. Louis de Montfort says in his book *True Devotion to Mary*, by this practice of entrusting yourself to Mary, "you will give Jesus more glory in a month than by any other practice, however difficult, in many years." And best of all, according to de Montfort, the road to holiness with Mary is "easy" compared to other paths. The great saint of Marian consecration writes that our good Mother "prepares her servants' crosses with so much maternal sweetness and pure love as to make them gladly acceptable, no matter how bitter they may be in themselves."

So Marian consecration truly is one of the best ways to avoid Purgatory and get a direct flight to Heaven.

2. Marian Consecration is one of the best ways to help souls get out of Purgatory

Why? How does this work? Well, part of Marian consecration means that we give to Mary "even the value of our good actions." This includes our merits, which we can "offer up" for the souls in Purgatory. For instance, if I have a cold or a toothache, I can offer it up as an efficacious prayer for the souls in Purgatory. But maybe you're asking yourself, "How does this help the souls in Purgatory?" It helps them because when we give all our merits to Mary, she augments them so there's more to go around. Saint Louis de Montfort offers an unforgettable image to explain this:

> It is as if a peasant, wishing to gain the friendship and benevolence of the king, went to the queen and presented her with a fruit which was his whole revenue, in order that she might present it to the king. The queen, having accepted the poor little offering from the peasant, would place the fruit on a large and beautiful dish of gold, and so, on the peasant's behalf, would present it to the king. Then the fruit, however unworthy in itself to be a king's present, would become worthy of his majesty because of the dish of gold on which it rested and the person who presented it (*True Devotion*, n. 147).

Like the queen in de Montfort's analogy, Mary purifies all our good actions, making them even more pleasing to her Son. So, when we're consecrated to her, all our prayers and good actions have even greater power and can be used even more effectively for the souls in Purgatory.

Now, here's one objection that might come up: When we're consecrated to Mary, because we give her all the value of our good actions, we, therefore, cannot apply our prayers to whomever we want and whenever we want. This is true. Let me explain: When one makes a total consecration of himself to Jesus through

Mary, he can no longer insist on determining who receives the value of his prayers and good actions. Indeed, the very nature of Marian consecration is that we leave everything up to Mary: We give her all, "even the value of all our good actions." Does this mean that Mary will forget the souls in Purgatory? Not at all. Does it mean we can no longer pray for the souls in Purgatory? Not at all. We still can and should pray for them — we should tell Mary of the people and intentions on our hearts. Then we offer her our prayers and good actions, letting her distribute the graces in the best way possible.

Mary is never outdone in generosity. When she sees that we give her the value of all our good actions, then in her generosity, she'll take care of our loved ones even better than we ourselves can! This includes our loved ones who are in Purgatory. Moreover, if we have a special devotion to the souls in Purgatory, and desire that they especially receive relief from our prayers and sacrifices, Mary will see to it that they are particularly cared for. Remember, when our merits pass through Mary's hands, they have even greater spiritual power, there's more grace to go around, and she'll give special attention to the intentions we hold in our hearts.

Consecrating ourselves to Mary, therefore, is a win-win. We win in that it's the quickest, easiest, surest, and most perfect way to holiness. The souls in Purgatory win because, if they're on our hearts, Mary is not outdone in generosity and will take care of them even better than we ourselves can.

To learn more about Marian consecration, I encourage you to read my book, *33 Days to Morning Glory: A Do-It-Yourself Retreat in Preparation for Marian Consecration* (Marian Press, 2013), which is an easy-to-use, step-by-step guide to consecrating oneself to Jesus through Mary.

Fatima and the Holy Souls

By Chris Sparks

I asked Chris Sparks, editor of our Thirteenth of the Month Club newsletter, to write about Fatima and how it ties into praying for the Holy Souls in Purgatory:

It may be one of the most disconcerting moments recorded in the course of the apparitions of Our Lady at Fatima, Portugal.

On May 13, 1917, during the first apparition to the three shepherd children, the eldest visionary, Lucia dos Santos, asked the Blessed Mother about two of her friends who had died. The Lady responded that one was in Heaven, but the other, Amelia, would be in Purgatory until the end of the world.

How can this be?

Keep in mind that prophecy and private revelation often speak in terms of things that will be — *unless*. For instance, in the biblical Book of Jonah, the Prophet Jonah goes to the people of Nineveh and tells them that in 40 days, their city will be destroyed. And so Nineveh would have been destroyed — except that the Ninevites heard Jonah's words, were struck to the heart, and responded by doing penance in sackcloth and ashes. So God, in His infinite love and mercy, forbore to smite the people.

Another example of prophecy mitigated by prayer and sacrifice is the repeated proclamation throughout Christian history that the end is near, and that people should repent and prepare themselves for Christ's Second and Final Coming. Occasionally, great saints such as St. Vincent Ferrer have proclaimed that theirs was the time of the end. And yet here we are today. What happened? Probably, people responded with penance for their sins as the Lord God wished, or else He in His mercy withheld the time of the end so as to give us time to repent and be saved.

So when Our Lady told Lucia that Amelia would be in Purgatory until the end of the world, perhaps that information was intended to help spur on Lucia and those whom she would tell about Our Lady's apparitions to pray, fast, and offer suffrages on behalf of Amelia and all those who, like her, owe a great debt of temporal punishment due to sin.

After all, one of the key elements of the message of Fatima is the summons to make reparation for our sins and the sins of others, to become conduits of the mercy of God so that, if we can help it, no soul will be lost. Our Lady showed the visionaries the fires of hell in order to prompt them and all true children of Mary to pray and offer penance for the conversion of sinners.

> You see Hell, where the souls of poor sinners go. To save them God wishes to establish in the world the devotion to my Immaculate Heart. If they do what I will tell you, many souls will be saved, and there will be peace.

So let us offer our sufferings and prayers to the Lord Jesus through the hands of Our Lady of Fatima for the Holy Souls in Purgatory and poor sinners on earth. As St. Stanislaus Papczynski taught, "It is one of the greatest acts of charity to pray earnestly to God for the freedom of the souls remaining in Purgatory," because they cannot pray for themselves. But how many poor sinners are in danger of Purgatory — or even worse, of hell — who will not raise a prayer for themselves?

So let us pray for the living as well as the dead, for the poor sinners on earth and the Holy Souls in Purgatory, in obedience to Our Lady of Fatima's call for reparation and prayer. She asked especially for the daily Rosary for peace in the world, a peace that can only come through our conversion and sanctification by the grace of God.

Our Lady also asked for the Five First Saturdays of Reparation, which she explained to then-Sr. Lucia dos Santos on December 10, 1925, in the following way:

> See, my daughter, my Heart encircled by thorns with which ungrateful men pierce it at every moment by their blasphemies and ingratitude. Do you, at least, strive to console me. Tell them that I promise to assist at the hour of death with the graces necessary for salvation all those who, in order to make reparation to me, on the First Saturday of five successive months, go to confession, receive Holy Communion, say five

decades of the Rosary, and keep me company for a quarter of an hour, meditating on the ... mysteries of the Rosary.

The practice of the First Saturdays consists of doing the following elements, performed with the intention of reparation, for five consecutive months:

- Confession (shortly before or after the First Saturday — so long as the person receives Holy Communion in a state of grace);

- Holy Communion received on the First Saturday;

- the Holy Rosary, five decades recited sometime during the day; and

- meditating for 15 minutes on the Mysteries of the Rosary (one or more).

Our Lady and the Angel of Peace also gave the child visionaries several prayers that we can use to great effect.

We can pray the "Pardon Prayer" for poor sinners who are still living:

My God, I believe, I adore, I hope, and I love You! I beg pardon for those who do not believe, do not adore, do not hope, and do not love You.

We can offer the "Angel's Prayer" in reparation for sins and for the conversion of poor sinners:

O most Holy Trinity, Father, Son, and Holy Spirit, I adore You profoundly. I offer You the most Precious Body, Blood, Soul, and Divinity of Jesus Christ, present in all the tabernacles of the world, in reparation for the outrages, sacrileges, and indifference by which He is offended. By the infinite merits of the Sacred Heart of Jesus and the Immaculate Heart of Mary, I beg the conversion of poor sinners.

We can offer the "Eucharistic Prayer" as an act of love for God and a way of gaining graces for the suffering souls in Purgatory:

Most Holy Trinity, I adore You! My God, my God, I love You in the Most Blessed Sacrament.

We can offer the "Sacrifice Prayer" when we offer some form of mortification or suffering for the conversion of poor sinners or for graces for the Holy Souls:

O Jesus, it is for love of You, for the conversion of poor sinners, and in reparation for the offenses committed against the Immaculate Heart of Mary.

Our Lady asked for the "Fatima Prayer" to be included at the end of each decade of the Rosary:

O my Jesus, forgive us our sins; save us from the fires of hell. Lead all souls to Heaven, especially those in most need of Thy mercy.

Let us pray for Amelia and all those who languish in the pains of Purgatory, for they cannot pray for themselves. Let us do penance for our sins and the sins of the whole world, for the many souls who are in bondage to sin and blinded to their own condition, and so will not make a move to take the Lord's offered salvation unless we help them.

I hope you have been inspired to pray for the Holy Souls. To learn more about the message of Fatima, visit ShopMercy.org and check out Fr. Michael Gaitley, MIC's *The Second Greatest Story Ever Told: Now Is the Time of Mercy* (Marian Press, 2015) or *Fatima for Today: The Urgent Marian Message of Hope* (Ignatius Press, 2011) by Fr. Andrew Apostoli, CFR.

Chapter 9
SAINT STANISLAUS PAPCZYNSKI

I'd like to share with you the deep devotion St. Stanislaus Papczynski (1631-1701), the Founder of the Marian Fathers of the Immaculate Conception, had for the Holy Souls in Purgatory.

My hope is that after reading about the example St. Stanislaus gave to us, you, too, might develop an even more ardent desire to aid those who are suffering and need our help to get to Heaven.

During St. Stanislaus' life, Poland was constantly at war with the Muscovites, Cossacks, Turks, Tartars, and Swedes. He himself accompanied Polish troops as a chaplain in battles against Turkey in Ukraine in 1674. He witnessed the carnage and saw many soldiers and innocent civilians die without receiving the Sacraments. Realizing that most of them were unprepared to meet God, he was moved to remember them in prayer, especially at Holy Mass. There is even testimony that in 1675, during the war against the Turks, the souls of the fallen soldiers would appear to him, begging for his intercession before God.

After further reflection, St. Stanislaus began to include in his prayers those who died from the pestilence that usually followed wars. He would devote his Masses, prayers, mortifications, penances, and all kinds of works of mercy to the Holy Souls, and he always encouraged others to do the same, especially the members of his Congregation.

Later, his mystical experiences intensified his devotion for the Holy Souls in Purgatory as he grew to understand how much they suffer. He would pray for hours, sometimes spending the entire night in the chapel. There, he would descend in spirit into Purgatory and stay with the Holy Souls, praying for them the entire time.

The first of St. Stanislaus' two well-documented visions of Purgatory occurred at the court of Polish noble Jacob Karski. One day, after saying Holy Mass upon the death of Karski's parents, St. Stanislaus was about to have dinner when he fell into an ecstasy. Then, after a while, he regained his senses. Despite the table in front of him being set for a sumptuous meal, he stood up and walked out the door. He then ordered the coachman to take him back to his monastery. There, his confreres were surprised to see him back so quickly and asked him what was the matter. He said to them, "Pray, brethren, for the souls who suffer in Purgatory, for they suffer unbearably!" Then he went to his room and locked himself in, staying there without food or drink for many days and ardently praying for the Holy Souls.

When St. Stanislaus preached or talked about the suffering that souls go through while in Purgatory, he would often have tears in his eyes and tremble at the thought of their awful torments. He claimed that there were so many souls in Purgatory that their number was far beyond the population of the living.

Those who knew him testified that whenever he fell into an ecstasy, he was in Purgatory taking on the suffering of the souls who were there. Saint Stanislaus wrote that he would ask God to increase his sufferings on earth so that he could help as many souls as possible. He offered all of his illnesses, pains, labors, persecutions, mortifications, and all his pious works in sacrifice for the Holy Souls. He did it all through the intercession of the Blessed Virgin Mary, whom he called the Merciful Protectress of the Souls in Purgatory.

The second vision came in 1676. Saint Stanislaus made a pilgrimage to the Shrine of Our Lady of Studzianna, and while there, he fell gravely ill. After Confession and Holy Mass, he felt he was losing all his strength and senses. He asked to be taken to a monastic cell. While appearing half dead, he fell into an ecstasy, once again experiencing the suffering of the souls in Purgatory. The residents of the monastery came to his cell to see how he was doing, and he appeared dead to them. They actually began to make his funeral arrangements! After some time, St. Stanislaus came out of his ecstasy. He then received a blessing from his spiritual director and went straight to the church to deliver a heartfelt sermon on devotion for the Holy Souls in Purgatory.

He later told his confreres that the Blessed Mother came to him and asked him to return to life, so that he might continue to help the dead.

The contemporaries of St. Stanislaus recalled how it became habitual for him to lock himself in his cell to pray. There, falling into ecstasy, he intensely felt the suffering of the Holy Souls. He could be heard saying, "*O Clementissime Deus, auge mihi Dolores, et ipsis poenas minue,*" meaning, "O God of infinite mercy, give me more suffering and diminish their punishment."

I finish with a quote from St. Stanislaus' book *The Mystical Temple of God:*

> It is one of the greatest acts of charity *to pray earnestly*
> to God for the freedom of the souls remaining in pur-
> gatory, or to assist them by merciful alms as by various

other means. Quite impious and foolish is he who is not moved by their torments, and does not help those who suffer when he can. The Leader, Judas Macca- bees, just as vigorous as noble-minded, "took up a collection among all his soldiers, amounting to two thousand silver drachmas, which he sent to Jerusalem to provide for an expiatory sacrifice. In doing this he acted in a very excellent and noble way, inasmuch as he had the resurrection of the dead in view" (2 Macc 12:43). This was done by a man who was occupied with continual wars, which usually extinguish pity, and who may well have known that the Synagogue did not have as much power as our Holy Mother the Church to apply the merits of Christ the Lord to the faithful departed. What is appropriate for us to do; for us who can obtain much from Jesus, and have such frequent incentives to bring assistance to the souls of the faithful who are destined for temporary torture? Therefore, I am greatly amazed how it is possible that a Christian does not begin to feel deeply the entreaty of these souls who cry aloud in these words: "Pity me, pity me, O you my friends!" (Job 19:21). What about the fact that we shall have in heaven as many Patrons and helpers as many souls we have brought there, thanks to our help, from the furnace of purgatory! I do not relate many things on this subject; let it suffice to consider and follow what the Holy Spirit declared: "it is therefore a holy and wholesome thought to pray for the dead, that they may be loosened from sins" (LV, 2 Macc 12:45-46).

Visit StanislawPapczynski.org to learn more about the Marians' Founder.

Chapter 10

SAINT FAUSTINA

Saint Faustina and the Holy Souls

In St. Faustina's *Diary*, the word "Purgatory" appears 24 times.

When I go on the road for my parish mission trips, I make it a point to touch on at least some of these passages. I always talk about entry 20, in which St. Faustina recounts the time when her guardian angel took her to Purgatory.

That experience was the direct result of her asking God for whom she should pray. "Jesus said that on the following night He would let me know for whom I should pray." As it turns out, it was the Holy Souls that Jesus was asking St. Faustina to pray for. And that is when Faustina became more devoted to praying for the souls in Purgatory, saying, "Since that time, I am in closer communion with the suffering souls."

We can all strive to become more devoted to praying for the Holy Souls, lifting up brief prayers for those most in need throughout the day. In entry 274, St. Faustina mentions that, rather than talking so much, she would say more prayers for the Holy Souls. "Jesus wants me to use that time to say some short indulgenced prayers for the souls in Purgatory."

And in entries 346 and 692, she writes about offering indulgences for the Holy Souls:

> December 24, 1934. The Vigil of Christmas. ... I was allowed to stay up and wait for the Midnight Mass. I was delighted to have free time from nine until midnight. From nine to ten o'clock I offered my adoration for my parents and my whole family. From ten to eleven, I offered it for the intention of my spiritual director, in the first place thanking God for granting me this great visible help here on earth, just as He had promised me, and I also asked God to grant him the necessary light so that he could get to know my soul and guide me according to God's good pleasure. And from eleven to twelve I prayed for the Holy Church and the clergy, for sinners, for the missions, and for our houses. I offered the indulgences for the souls in purgatory (346).
>
> O Jesus, I understand that Your mercy is beyond all imagining, and therefore I ask You to make my heart so big that there will be room in it for the needs of all the souls living on the face of the earth. O Jesus, my love extends beyond the world, to the souls suffering in purgatory, and I want to exercise mercy toward them by means of indulgenced prayers. God's mercy is unfathomable and inexhaustible, just as God Himself is unfathomable. Even if I were to use the strongest

words there are to express this mercy of God, all this would be nothing in comparison with what it is in reality. O Jesus, make my heart sensitive to all the sufferings of my neighbor, whether of body or of soul. O my Jesus, I know that You act toward us as we act toward our neighbor (*Diary*, 692).

If you are looking for some suggestions of brief prayers you can say, one of the short pious invocations mentioned in the *Manual of Indulgences* is "Lord Jesus, in Your mercy, grant them eternal rest." Or you could say, "Have mercy on the souls in Purgatory, Lord," or "Grant them eternal repose." To any of these, a partial indulgence is granted (see Chapter 11).

Saint Faustina has visitors

Saint Faustina wrote about being visited a number of times by deceased religious from her own congregation:

> This evening, one of the deceased sisters came and asked me for one day of fasting and to offer all my [spiritual] exercises on that day for her. I answered that I would.
>
> From early morning on the following day, I offered everything for her intention. During Holy Mass, I had a brief experience of her torment. I experienced such intense hunger for God that I seemed to be dying of the desire to become united with Him. This lasted only a short time, but I understood what the longing of the souls in purgatory was like.
>
> Immediately after Holy Mass, I asked Mother Superior's permission to fast, but I did not receive it because of my illness. When I entered the chapel, I heard these words: "If you had fasted, Sister, I would not have gotten relief until the evening, but for the sake of your obedience, which prevented you from fasting, I obtained this relief at once. Obedience has great power." After these words I heard: "May God reward you" (*Diary*, 1185-1187).

Faustina talks about feeling, like the souls in Purgatory, "such intense hunger for God that I seemed to be dying of the desire to become united with Him." That's a continuation of what she wrote in entry 20: "I asked these souls what their greatest suffering was. They answered me in one voice that their greatest torment was longing for God."

Father Benedict Groeschel, CFR, used to say that when we die, we have an immediate personal judgment. Part of that personal judgment is God determining whether we are ready to go to Heaven, or if we are rejecting God's mercy and headed to hell.

Even if we know we have sufficient sins that we can't go directly to Heaven, we see Heaven in the distance, so to speak, and that causes us to desire it even more. The souls in Purgatory are tormented by that desire. It's kind of like standing in line for ice cream. (Feel free to think of something you really want, but I usually want ice cream.) The longer you have to wait, the more your desire for it builds.

In entry 58 of her *Diary*, Faustina writes about another deceased sister visiting her:

> One night, a sister who had died two months previously came to me. She was a sister of the first choir. I saw her in a terrible condition, all in flames with her face painfully distorted. This lasted only a short time, and then she disappeared. A shudder went through my soul because I did not know whether she was suffering in purgatory or in hell. Nevertheless, I redoubled my prayers for her. The next night she came again, but I saw her in an even more horrible state, in the midst of flames which were even more intense, and despair was written all over her face. I was astonished to see her in a worse condition after the prayers I had offered for her, and I asked, "Haven't my prayers helped you?" She answered that my prayers had not helped her and that nothing would help her. I said to her, "And the prayers which the whole community has offered for you, have they not been any help to you?" She said no, that these prayers had helped some other souls.

I replied, "If my prayers are not helping you, Sister, please stop coming to me." She disappeared at once. Despite this, I kept on praying.

After some time she came back again to me during the night, but already her appearance had changed. There were no longer any flames, as there had been before, and her face was radiant, her eyes beaming with joy. She told me that I had a true love for my neighbor and that many other souls had profited from my prayers. She urged me not to cease praying for the souls in purgatory, and she added that she herself would not remain there much longer. How astounding are the decrees of God!

Saint Faustina's confessor, Blessed Michael Sopocko, speculated that the reason why this sister was in Purgatory for such an extended period of time was that she had failed to show charity toward souls in Purgatory to whom she owed prayers. Because she hadn't done the works of charity she should have done, when she died, the charity done for her was, so to speak, "shifted" to the ones for whom she should have prayed. That's why she had a greater debt to pay in Purgatory. It kind of goes back to Luke 12:48: "Much will be required of the person entrusted with much, and still more will be demanded of the person entrusted with more." This sister had received many graces and insights as a religious woman, but she hadn't shown the charity that those graces and insights should have compelled her to live.

Sometimes St. Faustina had encounters with souls in Purgatory that were quite brief:

When the soul of a certain young lady came to me one night, she made me aware of her presence, and made known to me that she needed my prayer. I prayed for a while, but her spirit did not leave me. Then I thought to myself, "If you are a good spirit, leave me in peace, and the indulgences I will gain tomorrow will be for you." At that moment, the spirit left my room, and I recognized that she was in purgatory (*Diary,* 1723).

After these visits from suffering souls, the thought of the Church Suffering often weighed heavily on her heart. On two occasions, St. Faustina asked Jesus to show mercy toward the souls in Purgatory:

> Three requests on the day of my perpetual vows. Jesus, I know that today You will refuse me nothing. … Third request: Jesus, I plead with You for the souls that are most in need of prayer. I plead for the dying; be merciful to them. I also beg You, Jesus, to free all souls from purgatory (*Diary,* 240).

Most Merciful Jesus, You Yourself have said that You desire mercy; so I bring into the abode of Your Most Compassionate Heart the souls in purgatory, souls who are very dear to You, and yet, who must make retribution to Your justice. May the streams of Blood and Water which gushed forth from Your Heart put out the flames of the purifying fire, that in that place, too, the power of Your mercy may be praised.

> From that terrible heat of the cleansing fire
> Rises a plaint to Your mercy,
> And they receive comfort, refreshment, relief
> In the stream of mingled Blood and Water.

Eternal Father, turn Your merciful gaze upon the souls suffering in purgatory, who are enfolded in the Most Compassionate Heart of Jesus. I beg You, by the sorrowful Passion of Jesus Your Son, and by all the bitterness with which His most sacred Soul was flooded, manifest Your mercy to the souls who are under Your just scrutiny. Look upon them in no other way than through the Wounds of Jesus, Your dearly beloved Son; for we firmly believe that there is no limit to Your goodness and compassion (*Diary,* 1227).

While we probably don't receive such visits, as I have mentioned in the past, those knocks and noises in the night could be the souls in Purgatory reminding us to pray for them. As apostles of Divine Mercy, we should be mindful of the Holy Souls' need for our prayers and the graces available through our devotional practices and other good works.

Saint Faustina and her fellow religious

Now, we'll explore why some of Faustina's fellow religious would need to spend time in Purgatory, as we continue to examine the passages related to Purgatory in her *Diary*.

In entry 1382, Faustina writes about Sr. Dominic:

> When Sister Dominic died at about one o'clock in the night, she came to me and gave me to know that she was dead. I prayed fervently for her. In the morning, the sisters told me that she was no longer alive, and I replied that I knew, because she had visited me. The sister infirmarian [Sister Chrysostom] asked me to help dress her. And then when I was alone with her, the Lord gave me to know that she was still suffering in purgatory. I redoubled my prayers for her. However, despite the zeal with which I always pray for our deceased sisters, I got mixed up as regards the days, and instead of offering three days of prayer, as the rule directs us to do, by mistake I offered only two days. On the fourth day, she gave me to know that I still owed her prayers, and that she was in need of them. I immediately formed the intention of offering the whole day for her, and not just that day but much more, as love of neighbor dictated to me.

People often ask, "Why would a nun in a cloistered convent end up having to spend three days in Purgatory?" One of the interesting realities about the way our salvation works is that some souls are called to a higher degree of holiness than the rest of us. These souls are referred to as "seraphic souls," for they are like seraphim, the highest choir of angels.

In entry 36, Faustina records how she learned that even she had merited a day in Purgatory. Obviously, she was being held to a higher standard than the rest of us.

SECTION 3

TOOLS
of
MERCY

Chapter 11

INDULGENCES

Frequently, I am asked about acquiring indulgences to help the Holy Souls in Purgatory.

The questioner is usually a knowledgeable Catholic who is concerned about becoming too scrupulous. "Must I have a declared intention each time I offer an indulgenced act?" "Have I lost graces by not stating my intention to do such acts for the Holy Souls or for myself?" "What happens to those plenary indulgences that I did not declare were for me or for the Holy Souls?"

Well, according to St. Augustine, one of the greatest Doctors of the Church, "There is more grace available to humanity than humanity has the ability [with] which to respond."

Because of our fallen nature, there will always be an excess of God's love to which we fail to respond. Our Blessed Mother restated this to St. Catherine Labouré in the apparition of the Miraculous Medal. Our Lady said she had many more graces to offer humanity than humanity was ready to receive. To which St. Catherine said, "Then give me all those graces!" What a smart woman! Don't waste time by trying to apply for each grace. Instead go for *all* the leftovers.

With these thoughts to consider, I remind readers that often in the ancient days of the last millennium (when I was growing up), we were invested in the Scapular of Our Lady of Mount Carmel prior to First Holy Communion. On that occasion, we were to some degree encouraged to make a de Montfort-like pledge or heroic act of charity in favor of the Holy Souls in Purgatory by "offering up" all "the satisfactory indulgenced works of our life" and asking Our Blessed Mother to dispose of them as she chooses.

Then, later in life, I discovered St. Louis de Montfort's *Preparation for Total Consecration to Jesus Through Mary*, and I made a much more mature and emphatic heroic act of charity of all my indulgenced acts for the Holy Souls in Purgatory. I occasionally renew that offering. However, if you don't remember ever having made such an act of charity, I offer this prayer pledge for your thoughtful consideration.

Act of continuing spiritual resolution

In Jesus' name, I hereby make a continuing resolution of my general intention to obtain all available indulgences. I place the fruits of my satisfactory indulgenced works under the loving direction of the Blessed Virgin Mary, primarily for the benefit of the Holy Souls in Purgatory, to be applied as she alone determines, according to the will of God Almighty. Amen.

Now, if a friend or loved one should die and you desire to offer for the happy repose of his or her soul a plenary or partial indulgence, it would be necessary to direct that particular holy act for that particular soul on that particular day. However, it would not thereby be necessary to renew the general intention of your continuing spiritual resolution afterwards, as that would already be in place.

To receive indulgences, it is necessary to have at least a general intention of obtaining them. Having prayerfully made the above act, you will automatically accrue graces for the Holy Souls.

Plenary indulgences

Only one plenary indulgence may be obtained each day, unless one is in danger of death. (In this case, one can obtain a second one for oneself by the priest's Apostolic Pardon.) To gain a plenary (complete) indulgence each day, you must perform a pious work (e.g., pray a Rosary in common with others present, pray for a half hour before the Blessed Sacrament either reserved in the tabernacle or exposed for veneration, pray the Stations of the Cross in a legitimately erected place [church, chapel, or oratory], or prayerfully read the Scriptures for a half-hour).

The usual conditions

For each plenary indulgence, it is necessary to receive Holy Communion and to offer prayers for the intentions of the Holy Father (normally, that includes one Our Father, one Hail Mary, and one Creed). It is also necessary to be in a state of grace (no mortal sins) having gone to Confession (the Sacrament of Reconciliation) within 20 days of the pious act. (One confession could be sufficient for 20 days before and up to 20 days after; therefore, 40 plenary indulgences could be obtained by one confession. This is a noteworthy change that was brought about by the late Holy Father, St. John Paul II, in the Great Jubilee Year 2000.)

Finally, it is necessary that the pious act of the plenary indulgence be performed in a spirit that is totally detached from all sin, even venial sin. If anything is lacking, a partial indulgence results. Saint Catherine of Genoa said, "We seldom are as holy as we think we are; we often overlook our many attachments to venial sins."

Nevertheless, "We should continue to aim higher each day, that we might achieve some good," said St. Maximilian Kolbe.

Partial indulgences

While we do well to obtain a plenary indulgence each day, we should not overlook the partial indulgences that are more easily obtained and far more numerous. Any Catholic in good standing, with a properly contrite heart, while performing an indulgenced work, may obtain a partial indulgence simply by being in a state of grace and having the general intention of obtaining an indulgence.

While a partial indulgence is not as powerful as a plenary indulgence, amassing many of them could be enough to free a Holy Soul from Purgatory.

Partial indulgences can be thought of as spiritual appetizers, while a plenary indulgence is like Thanksgiving dinner at Grandma's home. Given enough appetizers, one can be satisfied.

Every partial indulgence has the potential of being the one that releases a soul from Purgatory. Upon his death, St. Nicholas of Tolentino was welcomed into heavenly glory by the souls whom he had released from Purgatory over his lifetime by his prayers and pious acts. They had also been praying for the success of his priestly ministry.

The Four Daily Plenary Indulgences

There are four ways to gain a plenary indulgence every single day (while in the state of grace, following the usual conditions). According to the *Manual of Indulgences* (USCCB Publishing, 2006, p. 41), the four works are:

- Adoration of the Blessed Sacrament for at least one half hour.

Eucharistic Adoration is the source of so many graces, we shouldn't even need the promise of indulgences to motivate us to make it a regular practice! To spend time with God Almighty in the flesh, to be still and listen to Jesus Christ, Divine Mercy Incarnate, perhaps hearing His words by reading Sacred Scripture at the same time — this is a great aid to holiness. As Venerable Fulton Sheen once wrote in *Treasure in Clay* (Random House, 2009):

> We become like that which we gaze upon. Looking into a sunset, the face takes on a golden glow. Looking at the Eucharistic Lord for an hour transforms the heart in a mysterious way as the face of Moses was transformed after his companionship with God on the mountain.

As we gaze upon Jesus, the face of Mercy, we are made over in His likeness; we are healed, set at peace, and gradually sanctified, if only we let Him work on our hearts, minds, and lives.

Besides all that, we can also gain a plenary indulgence for ourselves or for a soul in Purgatory each day if we spend at least half an hour in Adoration before the Eucharistic Lord and fulfill the usual conditions (listed above).

• The pious exercise of the Way of the Cross.

Through St. Faustina Kowalska, our Lord specifically asked for this, especially at the 3 o'clock hour, to commemorate the hour of His Death on the Cross (see *Diary,* 1572).

There is more merit to one hour of meditation on My sorrowful Passion than there is to a whole year of flagellation that draws blood; the contemplation of My painful wounds is of great profit to you, and it brings Me great joy (*Diary,* 369).

So aside from the tremendous graces we can already gain through making the Stations of the Cross, the Church also has enriched the practice with a daily plenary indulgence. According to the *Manual of Indulgences,* we must make our Stations of the Cross "before stations of the Way of the Cross legitimately erected," such as the stations in almost every parish church, cathedral, and shrine (as at the National Shrine of The Divine Mercy, for example). "According to common custom, the pious exercise consists of fourteen devotional readings, to which some vocal prayers are added. To make the Way of the Cross, however, it is sufficient to meditate devoutly on the Lord's Passion and Death, and therefore reflection on the particular mysteries of the individual stations is not necessary."

Further, "progression from one station to the next is required," but if there are a lot of people and it would be inconvenient for everyone to try to gather at each station, the prayer leader at least must move from station to station. "Those legitimately impeded" — for example, the sick, the imprisoned, or the elderly — "can acquire the same indulgence, if they spend some time, e.g., at least a quarter of an hour, in reading and meditating on the Passion and Death of our Lord Jesus Christ." The plenary indulgence can also be obtained by "other pious exercises, approved by competent authority, which call to mind the memory of the Passion and Death of our Lord, likewise with the prescribed 14 stations."

• Recitation of the Marian Rosary or of the hymn *Akathistos*, in church or an oratory; or in a family, a religious community, or a sodality of the faithful or, in general, when several of the faithful are gathered for any good purpose.

This is the quickest of the four devotions. Do you pray the family Rosary? Do you pray the Rosary with your fellow parishioners before or after Mass, or with friends or neighbors? If not, why not? Everyone can gain a plenary indulgence for the Holy Souls, following the usual conditions.

• The devout reading or listening to the Sacred Scriptures for at least a half an hour.

Imagine a Church in which every Catholic gives half an hour a day over to reading the Bible. Pope Francis said in his introduction to a youth Bible, "By the word of God has Light come into the world, and it will never go out. ... Let us receive the sublime treasure of the revealed word. So you have something divine in your hands: a book like fire! A book through which God speaks." The Sacred Scriptures have been an irreplaceable part of every major spiritual movement in Church history. We will not be renewed or able to renew the world without being steeped in the Word of God. So come — take, read, and be transformed, as St. Augustine was and so many others have been even up to the present day. Let the Light of Christ, the Word of God, illuminate your mind and your spiritual life. And, as a great side benefit, help set the Holy Souls in Purgatory free!

Allow me to offer a few of my favorite ways to gain partial indulgences:

• Making the Sign of the Cross

• Praying the Rosary (not in common with others)

• Raising one's thoughts to God in a pious invocation

• Adoring Jesus in the Holy Eucharist for a moment

• Praying any approved "Act of Contrition," "Come, Holy Spirit," "Hail, Holy Queen," or "Glory be"

- Participating in a three-day retreat (like the ones I offer during my parish missions)
- Attending a First Holy Communion Mass
- Teaching a catechism class
- Attending a catechism class
- Reading the Bible
- Fasting from a pleasure or privilege
- Renewing one's baptismal vows
- Visiting a church or a cemetery on All Souls' Day to pray for the dead
- Properly venerating a saint on his or her feast day
- Giving alms (helping the poor or homeless, either directly to an individual or to a group though an agency)

Indulgences in November

From November 2 through November 9, we can gain a plenary indulgence each day for the Holy Souls in Purgatory by devoutly visiting a cemetery and praying. But first we have to prepare ourselves spiritually (following the usual conditions) for gaining such indulgences.

Once we have prepared ourselves through the Sacrament of Reconciliation, the second thing we should plan to do, if possible, is to attend daily Mass and receive Holy Communion as worthily as possible. Remember that Mass is our most efficacious prayer for the Holy Souls, and during Holy Communion, we are as close to Jesus as we can get, this side of Heaven. What an opportunity to pray for our suffering brothers and sisters!

Next comes the selection of a pious act that is suited to our temperament and lifestyle. It may not seem so at first, but our natural temperament and prior decisions that have shaped our lifestyle help us to choose pious acts well suited to our growth in holiness. While I — a celibate priest living in a religious community with easy access to the Blessed Sacrament 24 hours a day — might choose to pray my daily Rosary by myself in front of the Blessed Sacrament, usually I prefer to pray my Rosary in community. Often that means I pray it in the car with my fellow Marian Fathers while traveling down open highways from one Divine Mercy parish mission to another, since that is my ministry. You may choose to gather your domestic community (even if it is only one other person, perhaps your spouse or child) and pray the Rosary in common at home.

Some people tell me that praying the Rosary isn't for them. It is certainly not the only means of obtaining a plenary indulgence. As I've already mentioned, such an indulgence is granted each day from November 2-9 for those who devoutly visit a cemetery and pray for the dead. If you are unable to make it to a cemetery, you can gain a plenary indulgence by reading the Scriptures for a half hour and meditating on the Word of God. This is well suited to those with a quieter temperament and requires no one else's cooperation. Or, if you have access to the Blessed Sacrament, gain a plenary indulgence by spending a half hour of prayer before the Blessed Sacrament, exposed or reserved, with others or alone. Or gain one by praying the Stations of the Cross alone or with others.

No matter what pious acts you choose, the Holy Souls will be eternally grateful. And finally, do not forget to pray for the Holy Father and his intentions for each indulgence.

Besides gaining indulgences for the Holy Souls, what prayers might be especially appropriate to recite for them during November? Along with the Eternal Rest Prayer, here are some other prayers you might consider:

Prayer for Deceased Parents

O God, who hast commanded us to honor our father and our mother; in Thy mercy have pity on the souls of my father and mother, and forgive them their trespasses; and make me to see them again in the joy of everlasting brightness. Through Christ our Lord. Amen.

Prayer for the Poor Souls

My Jesus, by the sorrows Thou didst suffer in Thine agony in the Garden, in Thy scourging and crowning with thorns, in the way to Calvary, in Thy crucifixion and death, have mercy on the souls in Purgatory, and especially on those who are most forsaken; do Thou deliver them from the dire torments they endure; call them and admit them to Thy most sweet embrace in paradise. Amen.

A Prayer for All the Deceased

By Thy resurrection from the dead, O Christ, death no longer hath dominion over those who die in holiness. So, we beseech Thee, give rest to Thy servants in Thy sanctuary and in Abraham's bosom. Grant it to those who, from Adam until now, have adored Thee with purity, to our fathers and brothers, to our kinsmen and friends, to all men who have lived by faith and passed on their road to Thee, by a thousand ways, and in all conditions, and make them worthy of the heavenly kingdom.

For the Souls in Purgatory

O Lord, who art ever merciful and bounteous with Thy gifts, look down upon the suffering souls in Purgatory. Remember not their offenses and negligence, but be mindful of Thy loving mercy, which is from all eternity. Cleanse them of their sins and fulfill their ardent desires that they may be made worthy to behold Thee face to face in Thy glory. May they soon be united with Thee and hear those blessed words which will call them to their heavenly home: "Come, blessed of My Father, take possession of the kingdom prepared for you from the foundation of the world."

Chapter 12

THE DIVINE MERCY CHAPLET AND PURGATORY

By Fr. Chris Alar, MIC

I've asked Fr. Chris Alar, MIC, director of the Association of Marian Helpers, to relate this story about how he came to pray the Divine Mercy Chaplet for his grandmother who had committed suicide — even though she had been dead for a decade:

My grandmother passed away in 1993 and at that time, I wasn't quite back into my faith. I had always been Catholic, but I had never really fully understood the treasures of our Catholic faith — like how we can pray for the Holy Souls. Well, one day in 2003, 10 years after my grandmother had died, I went to make a general confession, covering the sins of my entire life, to a priest, and he told me all about Divine Mercy and the Divine Mercy Chaplet.

I was intrigued by the Chaplet because he told me how powerful it is for the sick and the dying. So I told the priest, "I wish I had had this prayer for my grandmother 10 years ago."

And he looked at me and said, "God transcends time. God is outside of time. In eternity, there is no past; there's no future.

There's just one big, eternal now. Chris, God knew back in 1993 that you were going to be here today, 10 years later. So go home and pray the chaplet for your grandmother."

I was still a little unsure, so I said, "But, Father, she's already been judged. She's in Heaven, hell, or Purgatory, and I pray that she's in Heaven, but I can't change that."

"Oh, Chris," the priest said. "Absolutely, your prayer can be very significant for what we call the Holy Souls, the poor souls in Purgatory. Because what happens is all the graces from that prayer that you are going to do tonight will be showered upon your grandmother at the moment of her death, even at the moment of her judgment. The fact that it's 10 years ago to God means nothing. God is outside of time, there's no '10 years ago' to God. So, the grace of you praying for your grandmother will definitely be applied to her at the moment of her judgment," he said.

He also explained how powerful those graces are because there are some souls that may have despaired at the end of their life. This gave me hope because my grandmother may have despaired at the end of her life. He said, "Those are souls that especially need any kind of grace that can be showered upon them at that moment."

"Your prayer, even though it's 10 years in the future, will be showered upon your grandmother through the grace of God back in the time of her judgment which you think was 10 years, in your mind."

"Father, that's amazing," I replied. "So my prayers can cause grace to be applied at the moment of her judgment that will allow her to say, in some little way, 'yes' to God?"

"Absolutely," he said. "That prayer is very huge for that Holy Soul."

Then he went on to say that even souls that are in Purgatory — friends, relatives, deceased people that you knew — those souls may still be crying for prayer. They can't be released to Heaven until we pray for them, because that's the way the Body of Christ works. We are all part of the Body of Christ. And on earth, we have to pray for the deceased. And when we pray for the deceased, many times that will clear their debt of temporal punishment for sin, and those prayers will provide that soul God's grace to enable them to go to Heaven.

Then I asked him, "So you mean, Father, that praying right now for someone who died years ago can help them?"

He said, "Not only *can* it help them — it *will* help them. Sometimes souls continue to suffer because no one is praying for them. So your grandmother may be suffering if no one is praying for her."

After our talk, I ran right home and prayed for her. After I had said the Chaplet, I felt this rush go through me. It was a sense of peace. I got this feeling that my grandmother was now at rest, at peace, and had been allowed into Heaven. I'm not saying that I know for sure, but I just had this peace that the Divine Mercy Chaplet released my grandmother from suffering because of God's mercy — not merely because of what I did. But God's mercy allows us as the Body of Christ to pray for each other. I just feel that God accepted that prayer and my grandmother, as a Holy Soul, was released from Purgatory.

I am very grateful for this priest who taught me about Divine Mercy and to be able to help my grandmother in a way that is so powerful.

We the living have the power to help relieve the suffering of the dead. We can pray for them. They can't pray for themselves. So it is our duty as members of the Body of Christ to pray for the deceased, for people like my grandmother. Our prayers are offered in reparation for their sins, and then they can be, through the mercy of God, released into Heaven. But we have to pray for them. If no one is praying for them, in many ways they may continue to suffer. And I feel perhaps that my prayers for my grandmother were accepted by God as sufficient reparation, and her suffering was permitted to end.

Chapter 13

THE PURGATORY BOARD

One time, I got a phone call from a woman who had read about our Marian Founder St. Stanislaus Papczynski and the 50 categories of Holy Souls for whom he recommended prayers. (It is called the Purgatory Board.) She asked me if that was a complete list of all the possible categories of the Holy Souls in Purgatory.

Well, yes and no. He thought it was complete, as did his followers, the Marian Fathers. However, no list could be complete for all people and all time. I pray for categories of people who were unknown to Fr. Stanislaus Papczynski: fire department personnel, police officers, and their chaplains; theater workers and entertainers; the people who helped develop the insulin pump and other diabetic treatments; and so many more.

Why do I pray for these categories of people?

I pray for chaplains because I had a cousin who, as a Sacred Heart priest, was a fire chaplain. In fact, he inspired me to respond to my vocation to the priesthood. And when the events of September 11, 2001, took place, I realized that there were many who had died unexpectedly that day. Maybe they were ready for death — maybe not. But there were many who gave their all for the sake of those who were suddenly even more in need of their ministry.

I used to be the pastor of a parish in the Chicago area, and one day I was called to the deathbed of an elderly woman who worked at the Chicago Lyric Opera. I prayed with her, anointed her, heard her confession, and gave her Holy Communion. Then I sat and talked with her for hours. She told me about her years of theater work, both backstage and as an usher. She had dreamed about being a performer, but she resigned herself to the fact that she wasn't quite talented enough. Still she told me many charming stories, which, as an opera buff, I cherish. When she died, I went to her funeral, at a parish other than mine. There was a fairly wide circle of friends at her funeral. She had never married. She had no children. However, at the reception, I heard story after story of how she had touched the lives of so many different people. She had loved people as Christ would have loved them. She had ministered to them by her simple, humble life. I think about her every time I hear about a famous performer who dies. Maybe this is an instance where the famous need prayers more than do the humble.

I have been an insulin-dependent diabetic for more than 20 years. During the last eight of those years, I have been served well by two insulin pumps, my first one and the present replacement. I have no idea of the identities of the people who spent their lives developing these things. I am sure some must have gone to their final reward. My life has been greatly improved by the insulin pump. I ask God to bless those who made it possible and, if they are deceased, I ask Him to receive their souls into His heavenly glory because of the good I have been able to do, thanks to the good they have done for me.

Before I entered the religious life, I used to love going to auctions in the hope of finding a box that was "made for me." I collected boxes, mostly wooden, some tin. They included big ones, small ones, and some that came in odd shapes. And once they were in my possession, they stored other collections. I was a collector of doodads and such. But I wondered who had owned my stuff before I came to own it for a while. I had a coin collection, stamps, matchbox cars, rosary parts (more later), fountain pen nibs, ink bottles, sealing waxes, and stationery. As a Scout, I also collected medals, ribbons, patches, and pins as I went up to the rank of Eagle Scout. I pray for those who owned my things before I came to be their owner briefly.

Now, I find I have a grand collection of images of Mary. Back when I was a parish pastor, I had a group of volunteers who belonged to the local chapter of the Legion of Mary. They decided to make a display of various images of Mary in the lobby of the parish church. When they took the display down after a month, I got several statues and most of the pictures. It marked the start of a new collection! In a few years, I found myself surrounded with many seldom-known images. And what of those who had been familiar with these devotions, for which there seem to be so few devotees today? I pray for those devoted sons and daughters of so loving a Mother.

Which reminds me of my rosary collection. I got my first rosary when I was getting ready for First Confession. I wanted to own more than one. So I taught myself how to make them. God bless Lewis & Co. of Troy, New York. They sent me a starter kit with written instructions. Soon, I had a different rosary for each day of the week. I would like to think that my rosary-making skill inspired me to become a Marian priest. It certainly inspired me to make rosaries and send them to the missions — first to Africa, then to India, and on to the rest of the world. I prayed the Rosary for those who were too poor to own one. I prayed for those who died without knowing the truth of our faith, especially the truth that we each have a Mother who loves us so much and wants to draw us to her Immaculate Heart. I prayed for the missionaries who taught others to pray. I prayed for those who did not learn the truth, for those who were embraced by the truth, for those who were buried with the rosary I had made for them so that they would know I loved them as my brother or sister. I will come to know them in eternity.

So we will come to know in eternity those who have prayed us into the holiness we have attained by our cooperation with the grace of God. They include our ancestors who provided for their grandchildren's grandchildren, the priests and deacons who baptized us and taught us the faith, and those who taught, mentored, coached, and guided us through our education. They include those who made our clothes, served our food, brought us mail, milked the cows, caught the fishes, cleansed our wounds, set our bones, delivered our medications, cut our hair, or changed our diapers. Let us pray for them as they prayed for us.

Chapter 14

GREGORIAN MASSES

Some Catholics may remember hearing about Gregorian Masses from their childhood. Some may never have heard of them at all. What is this devotion, and why does it matter today?

Gregorian Masses are a special gift handed on from the treasury of pious practices of the Christian faithful. By means of Gregorian Masses, we have the opportunity to do a great work of mercy: Pray for the dead.

What are Gregorian Masses?

Gregorian Masses are 30 Masses, celebrated one each day at any church, chapel, shrine, basilica, or any altar by any priest (or priests) for 30 consecutive days as soon as possible after a person's death. Through Gregorian Masses, we pray for the deliverance of that soul from Purgatory. For information on how to arrange Gregorian Masses, please see the end of this chapter.

They are named Gregorian Masses after St. Gregory the Great, pope from 590 to 604. In his *Dialogues* (Book 4, Chapter 55), he tells us that he had Masses offered on 30 consecutive days for the repose of the soul of Justus, a monk who had died in the convent of St. Andrew in Rome. On the day of the 30th Mass, the deceased appeared to his brother and announced that he had been delivered from the flames of Purgatory.

As Fr. Edward McNamara, LC, professor of liturgy at Regina Apostolorum Pontifical Athenaeum, has explained, the Church has ruled in the declaration *Tricenario Gregoriano* (February 24, 1967) that "it is not required that the same priest celebrate all the Masses nor that they be celebrated on the same altar. Thus, if a priest who has accepted the obligation of celebrating the series finds himself impeded on any particular day, he may request another priest to take the intention for him."

"Likewise," Fr. McNamara continues, "it could happen that the priest cannot find a substitute and the series is interrupted because of an unforeseen impediment (for example, an illness), or for a reasonable cause (the celebration of a funeral or a wedding). In this case the Church has disposed that … the priest retains the obligation to complete the 30 Masses as soon as possible, but he need not begin the series anew."

The custom of offering Gregorian Masses for a particular soul implies trusting that, through the mercy of God, that soul is in Purgatory. This practice recognizes that few people are immediately ready for Heaven after death, but, through the infinite intercessory power of the Mass, a soul can be perfected by grace and enabled to finally enter into the bliss of union with the Most Holy Trinity — our God, who is Love Itself.

Our Lord tells us through St. Faustina, **"I demand from you deeds of mercy, which are to arise out of love for Me"** (*Diary*, 742). Consider praying for the dearly departed every day and requesting Masses for their blessed repose in the Lord. Through our prayers, we help set them free from the effects of sin that block their path into the eternal joy of paradise.

Why do we pray for the dead?

Our brethren in the faith, the Jewish people, have long had various ways of honoring or aiding their dead. The Jews mourned Moses in the desert for 30 days, for instance (see Dt 34:8). The great Jewish leader Judas Maccabeus discovered that a number of slain Jews had been giving forbidden honor to idols of Jamnia (see 2 Macc 12:39-41). Trusting in God's mercy, Judas and his army took immediate action to seek to assure that the slain received God's forgiveness:

> Turning to supplication, they prayed that the sinful deed might be fully blotted out. ... He then took up a collection among all his soldiers, amounting to two thousand silver drachmas, which he sent to Jerusalem to provide for an expiatory sacrifice. In doing this he acted in a very excellent and noble way ... . Thus he made atonement for the dead that they might be absolved from their sin (2 Macc 12:42-46).

Even to this day, the Jewish people pray for their dead. Among other devotions, they often keep *Kaddish* (offer prayers of praise to God for a fixed interval of time) for their deceased.

From the earliest days of Christianity, the Christian faithful have done the same, as archaeologists have confirmed by looking at the inscriptions on early Christian burial places, and as can be seen by the most ancient liturgical rites, which have always included prayers for the dead. Gregorian Masses hold a special place among the ancient prayers of the Church for the Holy Souls in Purgatory.

Chapter 15

PRAYER OF ST. GERTRUDE

By Chris Sparks

I'm often asked about the origins of the St. Gertrude Prayer for the Holy Souls and about our Lord's promise to her regarding the number of souls who would be released from Purgatory when she prayed it. So I asked Chris Sparks, the editor of our Thirteenth of the Month Club newsletter, to research these questions for us. As you'll see, the result is an inspiring reflection on the power of the Lord's Precious Blood:

One of the most popular prayers for the Holy Souls in Purgatory is traditionally attributed to St. Gertrude the Great (1256-1301 or 1302). In the long form, it runs like this:

Eternal Father, I offer You the Most Precious Blood of Your Divine Son, Jesus, in union with the Masses said throughout the world today, for all the Holy Souls in Purgatory, for sinners everywhere, for sinners in the Universal Church, those in my own home, and within my family. Amen.

The popular pamphleteer Fr. Paul O'Sullivan, OP, included it in a short form in his booklets *Read Me or Rue It* and *How to Avoid Purgatory.*

Eternal Father, I offer Thee the most Precious Blood of Jesus, with all the Masses being said all over the world this day, for the Souls in Purgatory.

(Both versions are acceptable; use whichever version you prefer.)

Father O'Sullivan noted, "Our Lord showed St. Gertrude a vast number of souls leaving Purgatory and going to Heaven as a result of this prayer, which the Saint was accustomed to say frequently during the day."

The prayer traditionally attributed to St. Gertrude the Great is one of a number of offerings of the Precious Blood of Jesus that the Church has used and cherished over the centuries. In Scripture and Tradition, going back to the time of the Fathers of the Church, we find repeated depictions of the saving power of the Precious Blood of Jesus (see, for instance, 1 Pt 1:17-19; Rev 7:14; Rev 12:10-11).

The Blood of the Lamb! It is by the Blood of Jesus that we are washed and made clean, that we are given life eternal and made holy and whole. Jesus paid the price for our sins and for our adoption as sons of God with His Most Precious Blood, the Blood of the Lamb of God, which takes away the sins of the world.

It is through the Body and Blood of Jesus that we receive our salvation. It's deeply appropriate that we would join our prayers together with the Holy Sacrifice of the Mass, much as we do with the Divine Mercy Chaplet, in order to offer the Father in Heaven the Blood of His Son in atonement for the sins of those in Purgatory.

That same blood that saves us also sanctifies us, washing us clean of every stain and effect of sin. The Eucharist, the *Catechism* tells us, is the source and summit of our faith — because Jesus is really present in the Eucharist, Body and Blood, Soul and Divinity (see 1324). Through Jesus, all graces flow. No grace comes except through Jesus. So when we offer the Precious Blood to the Father in union with the Masses said throughout the world daily for the Holy Souls in Purgatory, we offer a very powerful prayer.

But how can we make such an offering?

To offer the Father the Precious Blood of His Son in prayer

is an extension of the prayer of the Mass, an exercise of our baptismal priesthood. The *Catechism* (1119) tells us:

> Forming 'as it were, one mystical person' with Christ the head, the Church acts in the sacraments as 'an organically structured priestly community (*LG* 11; cf. Pius XII, *Mystici Corporis* (1943).' Through Baptism and Confirmation the priestly people is enabled to celebrate the liturgy, while those of the faithful 'who have received Holy Orders, are appointed to nourish the Church with the word and grace of God in the name of Christ (LG 11 # 2).

The whole Church celebrates the Mass, not the priest alone. Even a priest celebrating Mass on a deserted island would not be celebrating Mass alone, for the angels and saints in Heaven would be in attendance, worshiping the Lord. Every Mass is an act of worship on the part of the Church, the Mystical Body of Christ, offering a sacrifice of thanks and praise to God the Father by the power of the Holy Spirit.

So when we pray an offering of the Precious Body and Blood such as the Divine Mercy Chaplet, we are merely doing outside of Mass the same thing we do within Mass: uniting our prayers and petitions, our sacrifices and love, with the Eucharistic offering.

There is sufficient grace in a single consecrated Host to redeem the entire world, for Jesus is fully present in the Most Blessed Sacrament. So, too, is there sufficient grace in any consecrated Host to let all souls out of Purgatory. God's grace is only constrained by our own free will, our openness to Him in our level of sanctity and trust. As Jesus told St. Faustina, **"The graces of My mercy are drawn by the means of one vessel only, and that is — trust. The more a soul trusts, the more it will receive"** (*Diary*, 1578).

So, then, with greater trust, and greater faith, our prayers will have greater power. "Amen, I say to you, if you have faith the size of a mustard seed, you will say to this mountain, 'Move from here to there,' and it will move. Nothing will be impossible for you" (Mt 17:20).

The oft-repeated promise attached to the prayer attributed to St. Gertrude — that 1,000 souls will be released from Purgatory each time it is said — must be understood symbolically to refer to "a great many" or the perfect number of souls. The efficacy of our prayers always depends upon God's mercy and our cooperation with grace. Just as King David was forbidden from taking a census of Israel (see 2 Sam 24; 1 Chr 21), so, too, must we refrain from attempting to control God's grace, from attempting to take a census of the souls helped by our prayers. We shall only know at the end of the world.

So let us daily offer to God the Father the Most Precious Blood of His Son, Jesus, for the relief of the Holy Souls. They are awaiting our intercession!

SECTION 4

USING *the* TOOLS

Chapter 16

PRAYING FOR SOULS IN THE LITURGICAL YEAR

Praying for the Holy Souls during Lent

When I was a child, Lent was about two things: giving up something and attending daily Mass with my family.

You gave up something as a prayerful sacrifice and an act of penance for the sins of your past. It was a frequent topic of discussion among my friends and family. It remains a topic of discussion among more traditional Catholics even today. I sometimes cringe, though, when my Lenten sacrifice begins to sound too much like a belated New Year's resolution: "Lose weight this Lent, so you can fit into last year's swimsuit."

I did not attend Catholic school when I was a child. However, walking to school each morning, I passed our parish church. So, with a little effort, I could serve daily Mass before school began. It was something several of my buddies and I did in our tiny town. Come Lent, though, serving at daily Mass was no longer something I could opt not to do.

Every day during Lent, the family piled into the car and drove to church in style. While serving, I was under the watchful eye of my mother and of everyone else, who were just waiting for me to slouch. I was a boy. I slouched during long homilies.

Now, as a priest, when I think of Lent, I think of the three main activities or practices that the Church calls us to do during this penitential season: praying, fasting, and almsgiving. They help us prepare to celebrate the Paschal Mystery (the life, Passion, Death, and Resurrection of Jesus) that culminates on the eighth day of the Easter season — the Octave Day, Divine Mercy Sunday. All of this may also lead us to reflect on the Four Last Things: death, judgment, Heaven, and hell. In turn, those of us who are familiar with the Divine Mercy message and St. Faustina's *Diary* may recall words like these of Jesus to her: **"When a soul sees**

and realizes the gravity of its sins ... let it not despair, but with trust let it throw itself into the arms of My mercy, as a child into the arms of its beloved mother" (1541).

Take a suggestion from St. John Bosco and try to attend Mass more frequently. If you only go to Mass on Sunday, add another Mass to your week. Or, if the Mass times are not convenient, try making a visit to the Blessed Sacrament. Already attending daily Mass frequently? Make it daily! Already a daily Mass attendee? How about a Holy Hour once a week, or a half-hour visit? Saint Padre Pio told penitents to have a Mass offered for the Holy Souls in Purgatory. Cannot afford the stipend? Prayerfully offer a Mass you attend for the speedy release of the Holy Souls into heavenly glory.

Saint John Massias, a Dominican, is said to have released more than a million souls from Purgatory, chiefly by reciting the Rosary and offering its innumerable indulgences for them. When Our Lady appeared at Fatima in 1917, she asked that we pray the Rosary daily. She could have asked us to attend daily Mass, but she knew we were not ready for that difficult of a demand, so she asked for the daily Rosary.

Why do we excuse ourselves so easily from Our Lady's request? If you cannot pray the five decades at one moment, break the Rosary up throughout your day: Pray a decade on your way to work or school, another at break time, another at lunch, midafternoon break, the journey back home, or after dinner.

Already doing daily Mass and Rosary? Good for you and for the least of your brothers and sisters in Purgatory! How about praying the Stations of the Cross once a week for the Holy Souls? You could use our newly revised, expanded *Way of the Cross at the National Shrine of The Divine Mercy* (Marian Press, 2013), which celebrates the epic Eden Hill Stations through prayers, meditations, and stunning photos of the new Stations. The book includes the St. Faustina Way of the Cross, which is prayed at the National Shrine.

You could pray the Stations on Fridays or, better yet, every day of Lent. Those of you familiar with St. Faustina are aware that our Lord asked her, **"My daughter, try your best to make the Stations of the Cross [daily] in [the three o'clock] hour,**

provided that your duties permit it" (*Diary*, 1572). So, if your schedule permits it, pray the Stations every day during Lent at the Hour of Great Mercy.

Another way you can make the most of your Lenten season is to remember and pray for a particular departed soul each day during the 40 days of Lent. Set up your calendar for Lent and assign a particular departed soul to each day. Then check your calendar every morning and make a conscious decision to offer up all your prayers and sacrifices for that particular soul.

Charity, another valuable way to deepen our devotion for the Holy Souls during Lent, is only limited by our lack of imagination. If we are called upon to offer an act of charity, we should do it usefully. Not only should we do the act of charity to the individual in need before us, but we should mindfully offer this charitable act for the Holy Souls.

Saint Martin of Tours gave half of his cloak to a cold beggar, only to find out afterwards that it was to Christ Himself that he had given the cloak. How much more will Christ and His saints rejoice over our charity toward the Holy Souls!

Finally, use the opportunity during the Easter Triduum, which includes Holy Thursday, Good Friday, and Holy Saturday, to take even more time to pray for the Holy Souls and your departed loved ones. Especially on Good Friday, bring the departed loved ones you have been remembering to the foot of the Cross. Entrust them into the care of Mary, Our Lady of Sorrows.

Indeed, Lent is the time for us to redouble our cooperation with God's mercy through prayer (meditation on the Lord's Passion, especially by praying the Chaplet of Divine Mercy), fasting (from favorite foods, activities, and especially near occasions of sin), and almsgiving (deeds of mercy: actual giving of goods to those in need, words of encouragement, and prayer).

This understanding of almsgiving as an act of charity for those in need, which can include prayer, should encourage you and all your family, friends, coworkers, and fellow parishioners to think of praying for the suffering souls during Lent.

As I ponder the season of Lent and think of what Jesus wants to accomplish in our souls, I think of St. Faustina writing in her *Diary* about the conclusion of her last retreat and her last conversation with the Lord before she passed into eternity. "Thank you, Eternal Love, for Your inconceivable kindness to me, that You would occupy Yourself directly with my sanctification" (1779). So, too, should we thank the Lord for giving us the season of Lent for our sanctification, which can be like a 40-day retreat with the Lord.

It's worth noting that during Faustina's final days on earth, Jesus also reminded her: **"My daughter, let three virtues adorn you in a particular way: humility, purity of intention, and love"** (1779). Consider for a moment how important these virtues are to our own spiritual growth, especially during Lent.

Humility — All the Doctors of the Church point to humility as the foundational virtue upon which any measure of holiness must be built.

Purity of intention — As Catholics, we are always examining our consciences to maintain our purity of intention. Simply doing the right (just) thing is not enough. As Jesus told the Pharisees, who were full of their own self-righteousness, "God knows your hearts" (Lk 16:15). This call to purity of intention always brings to mind for me the passage in the *Diary* where Jesus tells St. Faustina, **"I demand from you deeds of mercy, which are to arise out of love for Me"** (742), reminding us that, to have integrity, our love of neighbor must flow from our love for the Lord.

Love — And that brings us full circle to the primacy of love. Even little children can understand and memorize the two Great Commandments, "You shall love the Lord, your God, with all your heart, with all your soul, and with all your mind. ... You shall love your neighbor as yourself" (Mt 22:37-39).

During the Lenten season of the Church Year, we are called to rededicate ourselves to God through deeper prayer, examination of conscience, and repentance from sin. By doing so, we prepare our hearts for the joy of Easter and the boundless graces available to us on Divine Mercy Sunday.

I encourage you to make more time in your busy schedule in Lent for the Sacraments, personal prayer, and acts of sacrifice. Especially participate in daily Mass as frequently as possible and make a good confession. Offer your prayers and sacrifices for the Holy Souls, particularly for your own departed loved ones and friends.

Seek the Holy Spirit's guidance for what the Lord is calling you to do in Lent. Consider whether any of the ideas I've mentioned would work well for you. As you do, keep the big picture in mind: Give priority to the Sacraments. Remember that Lent is an ideal time for penance, fasting, almsgiving, and prayer. All of these can be done out of love for the Holy Souls in Purgatory.

Praying for the Holy Souls in November

As we discuss November 2, All Souls' Day, and the November remembrance, in which we spend the month remembering the souls in Purgatory in special ways, I want to share some recollections of Br. Andrew Maczynski, MIC, who grew up in Poland. He shares about his countrymen's special devotion to the Holy Souls.

"Back in my younger days, November 1 was always a special day," Br. Andrew said. "I recall everyone going to the cemetery all day long. The first was a national holiday, and people would often travel great distances to visit the graves of their parents, grandparents, brothers, or sisters. It is like Thanksgiving in the United States. Everyone is traveling in order to put flowers and light candles on the graves of their departed relatives. It was an important custom then and is still very popular today."

"I remember even after I became a Marian, I liked to go and pray the Rosary for the faithful departed on the evening of November 1 in the cemetery. It was November, so it was getting dark earlier, and the cemetery presented such an amazing view with the candles lit on all the graves. It was a beautiful vision ... candles being lit by the thousands throughout the day. It created a halo over the cemetery. You could see candles burning even in the distance. It was a very moving, touching sight."

"It is very moving to realize people still remember to come and pray for the Holy Souls. They plant flowers, organize graves, and pray for the souls of their ancestors. It's very inspirational to see that happening. People do believe. I think it's a great witness to see the faithful united to the Church in this way. Those of us who are still fighting are seeking the intercession of those who are glorified for those who are being purified."

Praying in cemeteries for departed loved ones, especially in November, is customary in all Catholic countries. It's typical for the faithful to visit the graves of relatives and friends on All Saints' Day (November 1) and/or All Souls' Day (November 2). Weather permitting, Masses are often held in the cemetery, and then members of the congregation go to pray at the graves of their departed loved ones. Leading up to All Saints' Day, many people decorate the graves of their loved ones with flowers and place candles to be lighted on the Vigil of All Saints' Day. The candles then burn through the night. People call them "lights of the Holy Souls."

Of course, during the month of November, Br. Andrew and the rest of us Marian Fathers around the world join together to offer daily Mass, various prayers, and sacrifices on behalf of those in Purgatory. We remember in particular the most forgotten souls, the souls of our departed Marian confreres, the souls of our departed loved ones, and the souls of departed benefactors of our community.

Brother Andrew's recollections got me thinking about what Catholics in other countries typically do for All Souls' Day. As I researched this, I found the *Handbook of Christian Feasts and Customs* by Fr. Francis Weiser (Harcourt, Brace and Co., 1958). In the book, Fr. Weiser says it is an old custom in central Europe to ring the church bells at the approach of dusk on All Saints' Day to remind the people to pray for the souls in Purgatory. When the bells are heard, families gather, extinguish all lights except for one candle, and pray for the Holy Souls.

Fr. Weiser writes:

In the rural sections of France, four men ring the church bell for an hour on All Saints' Day after dark. Four other men go from farm to farm during the night, ringing hand bells and chanting at each place: 'Christians awake, pray to God for the souls of the dead, and say the *Pater* and *Ave* for them.' From the house comes the reply, 'Amen,' as the people rise for prayer.

In most countries of South America, All Souls'
Day is a public holiday. In Brazil, people flock by
the thousands to the cemeteries all morning, light
candles, and kneel at the graves in prayer. The deep
silence of so many persons in the crowded cemetery
deeply impresses the stranger. In Puerto Rico, people
walk for miles to the graves of their loved ones. The
women often carry vases of flowers and water, for they
know they can get no water at the cemetery to keep
the flowers fresh.

I also know that Mexico celebrates it as *Dia de los Meurtos*,
the Day of the Dead.

In addition to what Br. Andrew described in Poland, Fr.
Weiser writes:

> The faithful bring to their parish priest on All Souls'
> Day paper sheets with black borders on which are
> written the names of their beloved dead. During the
> evening devotions in November, and on Sundays, the
> names are read from the pulpit and prayers are offered
> for the repose of the Holy Souls.
>
> The tradition of devoting eight days in early
> November to special prayer, penance, and acts of
> charity has developed over time among the faithful.
> [Today, the Church celebrates this octave on November
> 2-9.] People call this particular time of the year 'Soul
> Nights.' Every evening, the Rosary is said for the
> Holy Souls by the family while the blessed candle
> burns for the souls. Many go to Mass every morning.
> A generous portion of the meal is given to the poor
> each day. Further, the faithful abstain from dances
> and other public amusements out of respect for the
> Holy Souls.

On All Souls' Day in countries where fishing is a key occu-
pation, the women from the families whose relatives have died at
sea sail to the area where they perished. There, all say prayers for
the departed souls.

Food has played a big role in the All Souls' Day customs of the past. Father Weiser writes, "The Irish would build up the fire, set the chairs round in a semicircle, spread the table with a clean cloth, and put a large uncut loaf and a jug of water out for the Holy Souls."

Father Weiser continues:

> Catholics in Germany, Belgium, France, Austria, Spain, Italy, Hungary, and in the Slavic countries baked special 'All Souls' Bread' in honor of the Holy Souls and bestowed them on children and the poor.
>
> In Eastern Europe, the farmers held a solemn meal on the evening of All Souls' Day, with empty seats and plates ready for the souls of departed relatives. Members of the family put parts of the dinner onto the plates. These portions were not touched by anyone, but afterward they were given to beggars or poor neighbors. In Hungary, the people invited orphan children into the family for All Saints' and All Souls' days, serving them generous meals and giving them gifts.

As we prepare for the November remembrance, let's consider how we can adopt, or perhaps adapt, some of these traditions and pass them on to our children and grandchildren. May these practices help deepen our devotion to the Holy Souls and enrich our family life as we remember the faithful departed in November.

Praying for the Holy Souls at Christmas

As you gather with your loved ones in Advent and throughout the Christmas season, I'd like to remind you that it is the perfect time to teach your children and grandchildren about praying for the Holy Souls.

Why is it the perfect time? During this time of year, we are focused on family and friends, filled with the joy of the season and anticipation of the birth of the Baby Jesus. Now think of Purgatory, where our deceased family and friends are filled with suffering because of their separation from our Lord. Imagine the deep longing they must have to draw close to Jesus, their Savior! Even the greatest frustration that you ever felt as a small child waiting for Santa to arrive on Christmas Eve can't possibly compare with their yearning. This season of prayerful waiting and anticipatory joy, then, can remind us to sharpen our focus on easing the intense suffering and deep longing of the Holy Souls for Heaven.

A picture is worth a thousand words in this case. Consider the warmth and intimacy of a Nativity scene compared to the bleakness of Purgatory. According to many mystics, they perceived Purgatory as a very big space, filled with misty gray fog that looks like ashes. There, the souls are weeping and trembling in what seems like terrible suffering. The Blessed Virgin Mary has repeatedly told visionaries that these poor souls need our prayers, especially the ones who have no one to pray for them.

Remember not everyone believes in Purgatory, and certainly if you don't believe in Purgatory, you're not going to be praying for your friends and family members who have gone on before you. That's why we are so strongly encouraged to befriend these poor souls by praying for them. They desperately need our prayers to go from Purgatory to Heaven. And it is precisely these souls whom we refer to as the Poor Souls in Purgatory, because they are not rich in the friendships that will help them reach heavenly glory. All that said, we can rightly call all the souls in Purgatory the Holy Souls, because they at least know that their ultimate end is heaven. They are all on the way to the Father's House.

Here, it's helpful to keep in mind that Purgatory has several levels. The more you pray on earth, the higher your level in Purgatory will be. The lowest level is where the suffering is most intense. The highest level is closest to Heaven, and there the sufferings are less intense. Yet the longing burns even more earnestly in the hearts of these souls closest to Heaven as they approach their final end.

Some of the visionaries who have had experiences of Purgatory — not the least of whom is our own St. Faustina — tell us that the intense sufferings there are very real. But we always have to keep in mind that the sufferings are of a metaphysical nature.

They are contained in the mind and in the heart of the human soul. We only need to recall a horrific nightmare to get an inkling of how such sufferings in Purgatory might well exceed any here on earth. Just about every child knows how the horror he feels in a nightmare can be much more threatening and fill him with far more dread than anything he could possibly imagine after he finally wakes up. Given such suffering, it is a great act of charity during this season of God's peace and love to offer our prayers and sacrifices for the poor souls in Purgatory.

In fact, the Blessed Mother is mindful of how intensely the Holy Souls in Purgatory are suffering and how far each of them is from Heaven, since they are all her spiritual children in need. With a mother's keen love, she knows which soul needs her attention most. That's why she counts on the prayers and sacrifices that we bring to her to help the Holy Souls. Significantly, the Blessed Mother has also told us that many more souls leave Purgatory and go to Heaven on Christmas Day than on any other day. What a blessing! This is why it makes good sense to increase our prayers and sacrifices for the Holy Souls during Advent.

With this overview in mind, I'd now like to offer you some specific ways to keep your departed loved ones close to your heart during this season.

During the Advent season, offer alms in atonement for the sins of those in Purgatory. Almsgiving is one way to help ensure that you will start at a higher level, should you find yourself in Purgatory, but only if it is done with purity of intention in the spirit of charity. The amount doesn't matter as much as the disposition of heart of the one who gives it. We can all give spiritual alms: penances, fasting, self-denial, and physical suffering.

Another way is to place a special ornament on your Christmas tree in remembrance of the Holy Souls in Purgatory, especially for your own departed loved ones. The ornament could include photos of your deceased loved ones.

As you are sending out Christmas cards, include the St. Gertrude prayercard. The promise attached to the prayer attributed to St. Gertrude is that "a great many" souls will be released from Purgatory each time the prayer is said.

Send us the names of your deceased loved ones to remember in our daily Mass for the Holy Souls and for the intentions of the patrons of the Holy Souls Sodality offered by a Marian priest. Simply visit PrayForSouls.org/remember.

Finally, offer your Mass and an indulgence for the Holy Souls on Christmas Day. Especially remember those souls who are most in need of spiritual gifts this Christmas and are so forgotten and overlooked during these times of joyful festivities. Realize that the benefits of any indulgences you give to the departed come back to you.

If you want to remember a deceased loved one in a very special way — perhaps someone who passed away within the last year — honor that loved one by having Gregorian Masses said for the repose of his or her soul.

This practice recognizes that few people are immediately ready for Heaven after death, but, through the infinite intercessory power of the Mass, a soul can be perfected by grace and enabled to finally enter into the bliss of union with the Most Holy Trinity — our God, who is Love Itself.

Chapter 17

TEACHING CHILDREN TO PRAY FOR SOULS IN PURGATORY

By Fr. Andy Davy, MIC

I'm often asked by Holy Souls Sodality members about ways to teach their children and grandchildren to pray for the Holy Souls in Purgatory. Father Andy Davy, MIC, who serves as pastor of St. Mary Parish in Plano, Illinois, and who has worked in youth ministry for the past 20 years, has some helpful suggestions:

What if you could somehow arrange for an army of personal patron saints to look after your children throughout their lives? You'd do it, right? What if you could have your children perform one of the greatest acts of love in the process? You'd do that, too, right?

Well, you can. And here's how: Have them pray and offer sacrifices for the Holy Souls in Purgatory. Once souls in

Purgatory reach Heaven, they become the personal patron saints of the person who helped them be released from Purgatory. By praying for the Holy Souls, you, in a sense, get an army of saints who want to return the favor to you in some way.

In this chapter, I want to help you teach your children about this important devotion and show them how to create this army of personal prayer warriors, of grateful Holy Souls sped on their way to Heaven.

The Church teaches that the Holy Souls in Purgatory cannot pray for themselves. In Purgatory, where Divine Justice purifies souls, the prayers and sacrifices of the living — of us and of our children — can extinguish our loved ones' burning pain, caused by being forced to wait to be united with God in eternity, a delay caused by the temporal punishment due for their sins .

For children, this may all be a lot to take in.

Where to begin?

You can start by teaching them that *the greatest act you can do for someone who has died is to pray for them.* Start with the basics — that these children loved their grandma (or whoever has passed away). Focus their attention on their love for that person. Explain that this love doesn't end with death. Explain that when we are praying for our loved ones, we are keeping that connection. Encourage them to speak in prayer to their deceased loved one, saying something like: "Grandma, I love you so much that I'm going to be thinking about you and praying for you."

For younger kids:
'How do you bring up the subject of death?'

Well, kids are curious creatures. They will probably ask you about death long before you are ready for the question. Don't be worried that you'll traumatize them by talking about death. By and large, so long as we're honest with them, kids are good at coping with death and grief.

Focus on our Lord's love

You can remind children that Heaven is where we are going to be the happiest. It gives them hope. As a parish priest, I remind the children that our Lord loves the person who died even more than we do.

A wrinkled dollar bill

Next, since Purgatory can be a rather abstract concept for many younger children to grasp, I like to give them an analogy they can understand. Author Mark Hart asks:

> Have you ever tried to put a wrinkled dollar bill into a soda machine? You try your best to straighten it out but the machine simply can't receive it in its wrinkled, tattered state. But if you put in a crisp, new bill, the machine takes it no problem. Purgatory is where all the 'wrinkles' are purged and 'ironed out.' Remember, the wrinkled dollar is not worth less than the new one; it just needs some help. Put simply, Purgatory means you'll get to Heaven someday, but you have a few things God has to 'iron out' first. (Mark Hart, "Purgatory: Heaven's Waiting Room," *Life Teen* blog, November 18, 2013.)

Make small sacrifices

I like to encourage children to make small sacrifices for their loved ones who have died, such as saying, "I won't eat that second cookie and will instead offer it (that act of self-denial) for Grandma who has passed away."

At Adoration

I have them imagine that particular person who has died is cradled in their hands. Then I have them lift their hands up to the Divine Mercy Image of Jesus as they offer that person to the Lord. I have had kids tell me afterwards that they could feel the Lord telling them, "Don't worry." He is taking care of this person.

Going to their heart

Have them imagine their hearts are like a house where Jesus comes to stay. In that place, they can talk to Jesus about how sad they are that Grandma has died. They can allow Jesus to talk back to them. Have them think about what Jesus would say. Have them use their gift of imagination, through which the Lord can touch and anoint them. I've heard the children come up with some beautiful answers about what our Lord would say.

Prayers

The Eternal Rest prayer is great. You could teach them that prayer at the same time that they are learning the Our Father or the Act of Contrition. Another great prayer is the *Memorare*, because it allows us to commend particular intentions to God for that person who has died.

Plant a flower garden

The children can water their flower garden and pray for their deceased loved ones while they are watering. It will help them to visualize, "I'm doing something for Grandma."

For older children: Praying for the Holy Souls is all about love

Purgatory shows God's generous mercy. He does not leave us even in death; rather, He gives us the means of healing beyond the grave so as to receive God's love perfectly. Explain that the Lord gives us, the living, the honor to be a part of the healing process of the Holy Souls. What a beautiful act of love: helping our loved ones to enjoy perfect love with God!

'Maybe we are not ready'

Now, some children may not be ready to hear that Grandma might be in Purgatory and in need of our prayers. If you focus first on their natural love for Grandma and the love that God has for their departed loved ones, it can get them praying. It can also open up doors later to say, "Maybe we are not ready for Heaven at the moment of our death. The Lord loves us so much, He wants to help us get ready, even after we're dead."

Have kids imagine themselves as a Holy Soul in Purgatory

Have the children imagine that they themselves are waiting in Purgatory for help from the Church on earth. Then tell them that they have been forgotten. Let them picture what it would be like to be waiting, hoping that someone will help them get to Heaven. Then tell them that, because of one person's prayers, they are now in Heaven. Finally, ask the kids, "If you were that soul, would you ever forget what that one person, who maybe didn't even know who you were, did for you?" It really gets them thinking. They often say, "I would never forget that person."

Visit the cemetery

Maybe have them clean up and plant flowers around the graves of deceased loved ones. It will help them to understand, "I'm here at the cemetery, Grandma is buried here, and I'm praying for her as I put flowers here. I'm doing something for Grandma." If you don't live close to your departed loved ones, I'd suggest cleaning up and putting flowers around graves that have been forgotten, and saying prayers for the people buried there.

Tell 'ghost' stories

In our Catholic Tradition, we have many stories of saints being visited by the dead. Saint Faustina writes in her *Diary* of sisters in her religious congregation dying, coming back to visit her, and asking for prayers (see *Diary*, 58). It's helpful to get them talking about the Holy Souls, as long as they aren't tempted toward the realm of the occult. Talk to them about what the Church actually teaches about the tragedy of soldiers dying on the battlefield, many of whom are not prepared to meet the Lord. Maybe these ghost stories will remind them to pray for the souls in Purgatory and to say a prayer for soldiers.

Prayers

Teach them the Chaplet of Divine Mercy and the Prayer of St. Gertrude. They can pray during Adoration, the Mass, the Rosary, or at any moment throughout the day. And encourage them to offer up their sacrifices. They can offer their time, their exercise, or not eating that second piece of cake. The key to all of this is that they offer a prayer from the heart.

Many people worry that there will be nobody to pray for them should they find themselves in Purgatory. I hope these ideas have inspired you to help teach the younger generations about praying for the Holy Souls, and thereby make sure there will always be intercessors for them.

Chapter 18

HOW YOU CAN TRULY MAKE A DIFFERENCE

In this excerpt from *'You Did It to Me': A Practical Guide to Mercy in Action* (Marian Press, 2014), Fr. Michael Gaitley, MIC, explains how we can truly make a difference for a suffering soul in Purgatory:

It's up to us.

Imagine the worst prison cell in the world. It's stuffy, dark, and miserable. A man is stuck there and has no idea of when he can get out.

You know he's in there. In fact, his cell is right next to your bedroom, in your house. Every day, you pass by his locked room as you go about your business. Meanwhile, the guy inside is dying with longing to get out. It's all he thinks about. He doesn't eat, sleep, or drink. He's just there, 24 hours a day, burning with desire to be out of there, to get back to his wife and children, whom he dearly misses.

Now, as you walk by his door, he can hear the clanging of the keys on your keychain. One of those keys, which you carry with you every day, unlocks his cell door. You just have to take the time to stop, pull out the key, and unlock the door. If you do this, the prisoner will walk out of his cell a free man. And once he gets out, he won't have to go to a halfway house. Rather, his whole family is eagerly waiting for him right inside your living room. He wants to see them so badly, and all you have to do is take out that key and open the door for him. It's up to you. It's totally up to you. He's completely at your mercy.

Now, let's say you're so gracious as to take the brief time out of your day to open the door for him. Can you imagine that guy's gratitude? He'd do anything for you! Oh, and did I mention that his brother is your boss? Yeah, and when you let him out, he's going to embrace his brother and tell Him all about how generous you were for letting him out and all about how he would have been stuck in that horrible place for God knows how long had you not come to help him. Of course, he's going to tell his brother to help you in a thousand different ways. Night and day, he's going to plead with his brother until he rewards you.

I think you get the idea. It's so easy to help the souls suffering in Purgatory, and it makes a huge difference to them. I can't think of anything else that takes such little effort, yet immediately means so much to someone else. Perhaps this is why some saints have said that prayer for the souls in Purgatory is one of the greatest acts of mercy.

Now, if this mercy aspect isn't enough to inspire us to pray for the poor souls regularly, maybe the part about the reward of their prayers will. I mean, just as we cannot comprehend the suffering of the souls in Purgatory, neither can we fully gauge their generosity. The souls that your efforts release from Purgatory (or that at least bring them consolation) will be eternally grateful. From Heaven, right before the face of God, night and day, they'll pray for you and your family. And these prayers will be powerful. Praying for the souls in Purgatory is one of the best deals going!

Alright, great. So whether we do it simply from the goodness of our hearts or because we also like the idea of having permanent friends in high places who can pull spiritual strings for us — let's just do it. (I hope it will be for the former and not the latter reason.) Okay, but how do we pray for the souls in Purgatory?

Praying for the souls in Purgatory can be as simple as lovingly reciting one "Hail Mary" for them. And while that is certainly effective, I'd like to suggest five ways of praying for the Poor Souls, the "big five," that

I believe are the most effective for helping to release them from the prison of Purgatory.

FIRST, have a Mass said for them.

There is no more powerful prayer for the deceased than the Holy Sacrifice of the Mass. And while it's especially efficacious to pray for the repose of a soul while at Mass and to offer one's communion for him, having a Mass itself offered for one of the deceased is the most powerful of all. It could only get better if we were to have several Masses said for him. See your local parish secretary about having a Mass said or contact the Marian Fathers [1-800-462-7426].

SECOND, enroll the deceased in a spiritual benefit society.

Certain religious congregations have been given special permission from the Holy See to extend their spiritual benefits to those who are officially enrolled in their registers. This means that those enrolled can continually share in the spiritual merits of the Masses, prayers, sacrifices, and good works of a given congregation. One of the main reasons why my own congregation, the Marian Fathers of the Immaculate Conception, was founded, was to give relief to the souls suffering in Purgatory. For this reason, each Marian is required to offer up prayers and sacrifices for the deceased. Having heard of our mission, hundreds of thousands of people have enrolled their deceased loved ones in our spiritual benefit society, called the Association of Marian Helpers.

THIRD, offer an indulgence for the deceased.

You can get one soul out of his purgatorial prison, guaranteed, if you choose to apply your plenary indulgence to him. Now, the catch is the disposition of "complete detachment from sin, including venial." If you have that, then you can get a plenary indulgence every day under the normal conditions.

FOURTH, offer sufferings for them.

We all suffer. We all have a cross to carry, daily. The important thing is that we not waste our sufferings. We don't waste them when we unite them to the sufferings of Christ with love and offer them to relieve the suffering of the souls in Purgatory. We can also actively choose penances to offer for them, such as fasting.

FIFTH, pray the Chaplet of Divine Mercy for them.

We've already discussed how powerful the chaplet is, so this is a given. But here I would add that if you want to offer your chaplet for the souls in Purgatory, the eighth day of the Divine Mercy Novena has a beautiful reflection and prayer.

APPENDIX I

TESTIMONIES

Father Michael Gaitley, MIC

I was ordained to the priesthood on October 16, 2010. That means my first full month as a priest was the month of November.

That's the month dedicated to prayer for the Holy Souls in Purgatory, and it was perfect timing — at least for a new priest of the Marian Fathers of the Immaculate Conception. After all, a key part of our mission is to pray for the Holy Souls.

During my first November as a priest, I gave about 10 homilies about the Holy Souls in Purgatory and their need for our prayers. Preparing homilies about the Holy Souls got me reflecting more deeply on what our relationship is with them, and it had a profound effect on my spirituality. I'd like to share the key insight that stood out for me during my month-long, intense reflection on the plight of the Holy Souls: The suffering of the souls in Purgatory is exactly the kind of suffering we want to have, and the Lord is eager to transfer it from them to us. Allow me to explain this further.

Let's begin by asking the question, "What is the greatest suffering of the Holy Souls?" According to the testimony of St. Faustina, the greatest suffering of the souls in Purgatory is their "longing for God" (*Diary*, 20). In other words, once a soul is in Purgatory, it clearly sees God's goodness, beauty, and love, and this clarity makes the soul long to be united with God more than the most lovesick Romeo longs to be with his Juliet. But if the soul was not a saint during its time on earth, then it can't fully be united to God, at least not right away. First, it has to pass through a time of purification, and the longing for God itself is part of that purification.

There's another great pain suffered by the souls in Purgatory besides longing for God. It's the pain of contrition or sorrow for sin. In other words, once a soul is in Purgatory, it sees so clearly that it is because of its sins that it finds itself separated from God. This clarity is an agony. Imagine a time when you felt deep contrition for some personal sin. Imagine the kind of pain that David experienced after his sins against Uriah (see Ps 51). All that pain is but a faint shadow of the ache of contrition that the souls in Purgatory feel.

So, it seems to me that the two great pains of the Holy Souls in Purgatory are those of intense longing for God and agonizing sorrow for their sins. Now, wait a minute. Aren't those two pains signs of holiness in the saints? Indeed they are. The saints all experienced great longing for God in this life. They also had a clear awareness of their own sinfulness, and they were deeply sorrowful for their sins. In fact, the saints often had the gift of tears that resulted from their longing for God and their sorrow for sin. To them, the following beatitudes particularly applied: "Blessed are those who mourn. ... Blessed are those who hunger and thirst for righteousness [holiness]" (Mt 5:4, 6).

Do we want to be saints? I hope we can all answer, "Yes!" But are we saints? Chances are, most of us aren't. Well, then, it looks like the souls in Purgatory have something we want (great longing for God and deep contrition for sin). Yet we have something they want. That is, we can help the souls in Purgatory through our prayers and sacrifices. So, why not put the two of these together? Here's what I propose: Let's ask God for a kind of spiritual transfer. Let me explain what I mean.

Basically, the spiritual transfer works like this: In prayer, we ask God to transfer the suffering of the Holy Souls in Purgatory to us. Specifically, we can pray, "Lord, You see how terribly the souls in Purgatory suffer from their longing for You and from their intense sorrow for their sins. Well, then, in Your mercy, I ask You to give them some relief by transferring to my heart their longing for You and their sorrow for sins. Let my heart burn with longing for You, my God, and please give me a deep contrition for my sins! Amen."

That's a beautiful prayer, and I believe that the Lord is happy to answer it. For He is happy to relieve the souls in Purgatory of some of their pain, and He is happy to give us the grace to long for Him more and to be sorry for our sins. Moreover, the souls in Purgatory are also happy about this prayer. After all, it gives them relief!

Finally, we will be happy. Not only will the souls in Purgatory, in gratitude, pray more fervently for us, but the pain of longing and contrition is a beautiful kind of pain that makes us holy. Also, it's not a scary kind of pain. In fact, when we know the Lord's mercy, there's a kind of sweetness to longing for God and contrition for sin. And our merciful Lord will never give us more than our hearts can bear.

I'm so grateful that my first full month as a priest was the month of November. Now, the Holy Souls in Purgatory are particularly helping me to grow in holiness, and I get to help them, too.

Father Chris Alar, MIC

As a "Cradle Catholic," I had always heard that it was a virtuous practice to pray for our deceased family members and friends. However, for many years, I never seemed to embrace this kind of prayer. I thought the "faithful departed" were just that — faithful. Therefore, they didn't really need my prayers. I believed that since they had faith, they would make it to Heaven, anyway. My understanding was that some purification may be required in Purgatory, but, since all the souls there would eventually get to Heaven, they took a secondary place of importance on my list of prayer priorities.

Well, things completely changed for me after I graduated from college. After leading a "secular" life (to put it mildly), I moved to North Carolina and reconnected with my Catholic faith. During that time, I saw the zeal of northern transplant Catholics living in the South with the passion of Protestant Evangelicals, which inspired me to become active again in my Catholic faith. As I was trying to learn about what kind of prayer was "best" (vocal, meditative, contemplative, etc.), I quickly realized that it wasn't the *type* of prayer but rather the *intention* of the prayer that was most important.

After several years learning more and more about my faith, I began to hear the good Lord knocking on my heart about a possible calling to the priesthood. However, it seemed to me that God couldn't possibly use someone like me — someone with such a sinful past. But the Blessed Mother kept me close, drew me closer to Jesus, and finally gave me the grace and courage to say "yes," as she did with her *fiat*. During this time, my devotion to Mary grew, as did my interest in praying for my deceased loved ones and for all the Holy Souls. Therefore, it was a jolt of consolation for me when I learned about the Marian Fathers of the Immaculate Conception and how two of the major aspects of the Congregation's charism are spreading devotion to Mary Immaculate and praying for the Holy Souls. It seemed to be a perfect fit for me!

Consequently, I entered the Marian Fathers in 2006 and quickly learned more about this important part of their charism. Deeply moved by the death of my grandmother a few years earlier, I now embraced this kind of prayer — especially when I learned that these poor souls cannot pray for themselves. Then, during my novitiate year, I learned something that changed my life. I had always known that charity (love) was the most important virtue and that it was the surest way to please God, but I wasn't sure of the best way to live it out. As novices, we often discussed this topic — how to grow in holiness by means of increasing our charity. But again, I still was wondering, "How do I best do this? How can I be more charitable?"

It finally all came together for me during our novitiate meetings, as we learned more about our spiritual father, St. Stanislaus Papczynski. We learned about his passionate zeal for the Holy Souls, how he had a vision of the suffering they endured, and how he dedicated his life to praying for them, especially those who died in battle and of pestilence. But what grabbed my attention like never before was when he said that praying for the souls in Purgatory is one of the greatest acts of charity that we could do! At first, I wasn't sure why this was so, but after thinking about it, it became clearer to me. Wouldn't the most charitable thing we could do be to help those who cannot help themselves? When we help those who most need our help, that is the greatest form of charity. This realization was the impetus I needed to become completely devoted to the Holy Souls, especially after learning how St. Stanislaus had had a vision of the suffering they endure. The thought of my deceased loved ones bearing this kind of pain and suffering tugged at my emotions, and now I wanted to help them in any way I could.

As a result of this new inspiration, I quickly rallied a team of "Mary's Marines" at our Marian Scholasticate in Washington, D.C. I went to many of my seminarian brothers and asked them to join me in praying for the souls in Purgatory — to help them like a commando team of Special Forces parachuting into battle to relieve the weary soldiers on the front lines. This is what St. Stanislaus did! He had a special place in his heart and prayer life for the Holy Souls, and I wanted to do the same.

Many brothers joined me in this devotion, and often a team of us would go to a local cemetery to pray for the dead (especially during the first week of November when the Church emphasizes prayers for the dead, starting on All Souls' Day). This devotion has remained strong in my heart and in the hearts of my seminarian brothers who know how important it is to help our deceased family and friends.

Now that I have become a priest, I feel even more devoted to this cause. I know for a fact that the Holy Souls have helped me on numerous occasions, so the least I can do is pray for them and offer Masses and sacrifices in the hope of shortening their stay in Purgatory.

But God had more to teach me. Let me explain. In today's society, there seems to be an inordinate interest in paranormal activity. In fact, I myself have experienced strange occurrences that seemed to be unexplainable. When I first moved into our Marian House in Steubenville, Ohio, I began to experience strange events that some could interpret as spiritual disturbances, such as slamming doors, the sound of footsteps when nobody was present, and objects moving by themselves.

After bringing this to the attention of my superior, we had a Mass said in the house for all the souls in Purgatory, especially those who may have died in the house over its 100-year history. Much to my surprise, after this Mass was said, all of these strange occurrences ceased. It was as if these poor souls were reaching out for our attention — begging us for Masses and prayers! I believe these were simply souls who had no one to pray for them, and once we had had a Mass said, they were able to rest in peace. A beautiful sense of joy came to me when I realized our prayers could have such power.

Today, I often celebrate Mass at the Marian Helpers Center in Stockbridge, Massachusetts. It is an honor and a blessing to celebrate daily Mass for our staff and Shrine pilgrims who love the Lord and want to do His will. Recently, I began to lead the congregation after Mass in the recitation of the St. Gertrude prayer, which is specifically said to aid the Holy Souls in Purgatory. The response has been amazing, with several people telling me of their desire to help these souls in their need.

Therefore, I humbly implore all of you to please join me and all the Marian Fathers in our efforts to aid our brothers and sisters who have passed from this life and have entered into eternity. Known as the "Church Suffering," they are part of the Body of Christ. And as the "Church Militant" here on earth, it is our obligation to help them through our prayers and sacrifices. In fact, we should not see this as a forced obligation, but rather as a joyous act of love. And remember, with each soul you help to release from Purgatory, you continue to build an army of souls in Heaven that will aid and assist you here on earth with all of your needs!

Father Chris Alar, MIC, was ordained to the sacred priesthood on Saturday, May 31, 2014.

Father Thaddaeus Lancton, MIC

My parents, Our Lady, and the Marian Fathers of the Immaculate Conception have all shaped my devotion to the Holy Souls in Purgatory in important ways.

My mother passed away when I was just 2 years old. Then, by the time I was 18, I had lost my father and my grandparents. Yet, because my loving father had brought me up in a devout Catholic home, I knew it was important to pray for the souls of my deceased loved ones.

In fact, when I was alone with my father at the moment of his death, the first thought that came to my mind was to pray for his soul. I dearly loved my father, who had been such an example to me of the Heavenly Father's love. Nevertheless, I knew my father had had faults like us all, and so I began to pray the Rosary, asking for Mary to allow my dad entrance into Heaven from Purgatory.

During the Third Glorious Mystery, I had a mental "vision." I didn't see anything with my physical vision, but I could clearly "see" with the eyes of my soul my father rising up to Heaven's gates, where my mother was waiting to embrace him. This "sight" gave me immense peace and joy in a moment of fear and sadness. This moment also confirmed in me the importance of praying for the souls in Purgatory. I believe that my prayers helped my father enter Heaven.

In 2007, at age 20, my devotion to the Holy Souls deepened when I entered the Marian Fathers, a religious community committed to praying for the suffering souls in Purgatory, especially forgotten souls such as the victims of war and disease. I see this as Divine Providence guiding my life. Before I joined the Marians, I prayed primarily for deceased family members, but now I try to pray for all those who die on a daily basis (which can be upwards of 140,000 people per day).

Since joining the Marians, I also better understand how Mary Immaculate can inspire our prayer for the Holy Souls. Growing up, I would often pray the Rosary with my family, mindful of those who were about to die and of the souls in Purgatory. But it was during my formation as a Marian that I began to understand how praying for the Holy Souls is tied intimately to the honor God has given Our Lady in her Immaculate Conception.

I came to see that as we venerate God's gift of preventing any sin in her soul, so we pray that all of us may be cleansed of our sins and able to enter God's presence. As the collect or opening prayer for Mass on the Solemnity of the Immaculate Conception expresses it:

> O God, who by the Immaculate Conception of the Blessed Virgin prepared a worthy dwelling for your Son, grant, we pray, that, as you preserved her from every stain by virtue of the Death of your Son, which

you foresaw, so, *through her intercession, we, too, may be cleansed and admitted to your presence* (emphasis added).

So the gift of purity of body and soul given to Mary is extended by God to all of us as we are purified of our sins, either in this life or in the life to come. And it comes to us through her powerful maternal intercession, which is especially attentive to the needs of the suffering souls.

As a Marian, I have grown as well in my love of the Holy Souls by participating in the November remembrance, during the month when the Church especially encourages us to pray for the Holy Souls. On November 2, we commemorate All Souls' Day for all the faithful departed. Then, particularly during the octave after All Souls', we intensify our prayer for the suffering souls. For instance, we Marians typically find time each day during the octave to visit a cemetery so as to obtain a plenary indulgence for some suffering soul.

These observances also foster brotherly charity in our Marian community life together, which itself is a good antidote to Purgatory. Indeed, such charity illustrates one of the most consoling aspects of praying for the souls: the knowledge that there might be many souls in Heaven who are praying for me in my various trials, just as I prayed for them. Their prayers may help me grow in holiness so that I can enter Heaven quickly after my death. I believe that the souls of my father and mother are among the souls praying for me.

Father Thaddaeus Lancton, MIC, was ordained to the sacred priesthood on Saturday, May 30, 2015.

Father Allen Alexander, MIC

I have had a devotion to the souls in Purgatory since I was a child. I can remember at wakes and funerals always wanting to go up and pray before the body of the deceased. One of the first funerals I can remember clearly was that of my great uncle, who died when I was only 10.

Even at that age, I had a clear idea what Purgatory was, and I knew that I was particularly called to pray for the souls of those who had just died, like my great uncle.

From a young age, I also felt the call to serve God as a priest, possibly in a religious community. So around the time I started high school, I began to actively seek information from various dioceses and religious communities. I wanted to get a better sense of where God was calling me to go after I graduated. One of the reasons I chose to pursue my religious vocation with the Marian Fathers was because praying for the Holy Souls in Purgatory is a founding aspect of the charism of the Marian Fathers.

Just a short time before I began my search for a religious community, I suffered two significant losses: One was the death of my grandfather during my freshman year of high school; the other was the death of a young woman, a senior at my Catholic high school when I was a sophomore. She died suddenly due to unfortunate circumstances that took place while she and other members of the senior class were celebrating their graduation.

Both of these deaths affected me profoundly. I can remember praying the Divine Mercy Chaplet for both of them.

While my grandfather was dying, several of my family members and I prayed the chaplet at his bedside. I remember my grandfather quoting John 3:16: "God so loved the world that He gave His only begotten Son that whoever believes in Him might not perish but might have eternal life." Then, just before he passed, he said that he saw a light coming toward him.

After my grandfather died, I had the honor of serving as a pallbearer for his funeral, and I will never forget it. It meant so much to me. I understood in some way why it is a work of mercy to "bury the dead."

I also felt called to pray the chaplet for the young woman. I didn't know her very well, but I always remembered how nice she was and that I saw the light of Christ whenever she smiled.

I slept at my grandparents' house the night before her funeral. I could not sleep, so I prayed. And as I prayed, I felt her presence as if she were in the room with me. At least in my mind, I could see her.

I felt her asking for my prayers. So I prayed, and it was as if I saw her smile. In my heart, I believe that God allowed me to assist her to leave Purgatory and enter Heaven through His grace.

These two profound experiences with death helped to confirm my belief that I should join the Marian community.

Since joining the Marian Fathers and embracing their charism, my devotion to the Holy Souls has grown.

During my novitiate, I enjoyed learning so much about our Father Founder, St. Stanislaus Papczynski, and his profound devotion to the Poor Souls in Purgatory, particularly those who died suddenly as a result of war and pestilence. While reading about his experiences with the souls of the faithful departed, I felt as if we were kindred spirits.

My favorite story is that one time, during dinner, he suddenly stood up and left the room. After a while, he returned. When asked where he had gone, St. Stanislaus admonished all present to pray fervently for the souls being purified in Purgatory.

The first time I attended the funeral of a member of the Marian community — as well as each time thereafter — I was deeply moved by the devotion of my Marian confreres for our beloved dead.

On such solemn occasions in Stockbridge, Massachusetts, we chant the vespers for the dead and keep watch with the body of our beloved brother the night before the burial. In the morning, holding torches aloft and following the crucifer (the person who carries the crucifix), we process with the body in a simple wooden casket from the Chapel of the Immaculate Conception at the National Shrine of The Divine Mercy to the graveyard just a few hundred yards away. There, we sprinkle holy water and dirt on the casket before lowering it into the ground. All of these acts for our beloved dead speak to me of the Communion of Saints, which is an essential part of the Church as the Body of Christ.

I am also very fond of the continuous prayers for the dead, which are a special part of Marian community life. Every Monday that is not impeded by an obligatory feast or memorial, we pray the Office of the Dead, which is an arrangement of the Liturgy of the Hours that calls to mind the souls of the faithful departed and invokes God's mercy upon them. May they quickly rejoice in their entrance into Heaven.

During the month of November, these prayers take on even more significance. On the commemoration of "All Souls' Day" and the seven days that follow, we chant vespers from the Office of the Dead.

Many of us also visit the cemetery each night for the first nine days of November, usually reciting the Divine Mercy Chaplet or other prayers for the deceased.

Whenever I hear of someone dying, I now stop whatever I am doing and pray for the repose of his or her soul. I also make a point, as do most Marians, of praying every time we pass a cemetery and of striving each day to obtain a plenary indulgence for a poor soul.

One of my favorite prayers for the souls in Purgatory is the Prayer of St. Gertrude, which, according to a pious tradition, distributes graces to a great many souls each time it is said (see Chapter 15).

I highly recommend it, along with any prayers that you already say for the suffering souls.

May God bless you all for the profound act of mercy that it is to pray for those who are suffering in Purgatory and can no longer pray for themselves.

Father Allen Alexander, MIC, was ordained to the sacred priesthood on Saturday, July 25, 2015.

APPENDIX II

PRAYERS

The Eternal Rest Prayer

Eternal rest grant unto them, O Lord, and let perpetual light shine upon them. May their souls and all the souls of the faithful departed, through the mercy of God, rest in peace. Amen.

Saint Gertrude's Prayer

Eternal Father, I offer You the Most Precious Blood of Your Divine Son, Jesus, in union with the Masses said throughout the world today, for all the Holy Souls in Purgatory, for sinners everywhere, for sinners in the Universal Church, those in my own home, and within my family. Amen.

Chaplet of Divine Mercy

1. Make the Sign of the Cross

In the name of the Father, and of the Son, and of the Holy Spirit. Amen.

2. Optional Opening Prayers

You expired, Jesus, but the source of life gushed forth for souls, and the ocean of mercy opened up for the whole world. O Fount of Life, unfathomable Divine Mercy, envelop the whole world and empty Yourself out upon us.

O Blood and Water, which gushed forth from the Heart of Jesus as a fountain of Mercy for us, I trust in You! (Repeat three times)

3. Our Father

Our Father, Who art in heaven, hallowed be Thy name; Thy kingdom come; Thy will be done on earth as it is in heaven. Give us this day our daily bread; and forgive us our trespasses as we forgive those who trespass against us; and lead us not into temptation, but deliver us from evil, Amen.

4. Hail Mary

Hail Mary, full of grace. The Lord is with thee. Blessed art thou amongst women, and blessed is the fruit of thy womb, Jesus. Holy Mary, Mother of God, pray for us sinners, now and at the hour of our death. Amen.

5. The Apostles' Creed

I believe in God, the Father almighty, Creator of heaven and earth, and in Jesus Christ, His only Son, our Lord, who was conceived by the Holy Spirit, born of the Virgin Mary, suffered under Pontius Pilate, was crucified, died and was buried; He descended into hell; on the third day He rose again from the dead; He ascended into heaven, and is seated at the right hand of God the Father almighty; from there He will come to judge the living and the dead. I believe in the Holy Spirit, the holy catholic Church, the communion of saints, the forgiveness of sins, the resurrection of the body, and life everlasting. Amen.

6. The Eternal Father

Eternal Father, I offer you the Body and Blood, Soul and Divinity of Your Dearly Beloved Son, Our Lord, Jesus Christ, in atonement for our sins and those of the whole world.

7. On the 10 Small Beads of Each Decade

For the sake of His sorrowful Passion, have mercy on us and on the whole world.

8. Repeat for the remaining decades

Saying the "Eternal Father" (6) on the "Our Father" bead and then 10 "For the sake of His sorrowful Passion" (7) on the following "Hail Mary" beads.

9. Conclude with Holy God (Repeat three times)

Holy God, Holy Mighty One, Holy Immortal One, have mercy on us and on the whole world.

10. Optional Closing Prayer

Eternal God, in whom mercy is endless and the treasury of compassion — inexhaustible, look kindly upon us and increase Your mercy in us, that in difficult moments we might not despair nor become despondent, but with great confidence submit ourselves to Your holy will, which is Love and Mercy itself.

Memorare

Remember, O most gracious Virgin Mary, that never was it known that anyone who fled to thy protection, implored thy help, or sought thine intercession was left unaided.

Inspired by this confidence, I fly unto thee, O Virgin of virgins, my mother; to thee do I come, before thee I stand, sinful and sorrowful. O Mother of the Word Incarnate, despise not my petitions, but in thy mercy hear and answer me. Amen.

Prayers for the Deceased for Every Day of the Week

V. O Lord, hear my prayer.
R. And let my cry come unto You.

O God, the Creator and Redeemer of all the faithful; grant unto the souls of Your servants and handmaids the remission of all their sins: that through our devout supplications they may obtain the pardon they have always desired. Who lives and reigns, world without end. Amen.

SUNDAY

O Lord God omnipotent, I ask You by the Precious Blood, which Your divine Son, Jesus, shed in the Garden, deliver the souls in Purgatory, and especially that one which is the most forsaken of all, and bring it into Your glory, where it may praise and bless You forever. Amen.

MONDAY

O Lord God omnipotent, I ask You by the Precious Blood which Your divine Son, Jesus, shed in cruel scourging, deliver the souls in Purgatory, and among them all, especially that soul which is nearest to its entrance into Your glory, that it may soon praise You and bless You forever. Amen.

TUESDAY

O Lord God omnipotent, I ask You by the Precious Blood of Your divine Son, Jesus, that was shed in His bitter crowning with thorns, deliver the souls in Purgatory, and among them all, particularly that soul which is in the greatest need of our prayers, in order that it may not long be delayed in praising You in Your glory and blessing You forever. Amen.

WEDNESDAY

O Lord God omnipotent, I ask You by the Precious Blood of Your divine Son, Jesus, that was shed in the streets of Jerusalem while He carried on His sacred shoulders the heavy burden of the Cross, deliver the souls in Purgatory and especially that one which is richest in merits in Your sight, so that, having soon attained the high place in glory to which it is destined, it may praise You triumphantly and bless You forever. Amen.

THURSDAY

O Lord God omnipotent, I ask You by the Precious Body and Blood of Your divine Son, Jesus, which He Himself on the night before His passion gave as food and drink to His beloved Apostles and bequeathed to His holy Church the perpetual Sacrifice and life-giving nourishment of His faithful people, deliver the souls in Purgatory, but most of all, that soul which was most devoted to this mystery of infinite love, in order that it may praise You together with Your divine Son and the Holy Spirit in Your glory forever. Amen.

FRIDAY

O Lord God omnipotent, I ask You by the Precious Blood, which Jesus, Your divine Son, shed this day upon the tree of the Cross, especially from His sacred hands and feet, deliver the souls in Purgatory, and particularly that soul for whom I am most bound to pray, in order that I may not be the cause which hinders You from admitting it quickly to the possession of Your glory where it may praise and bless You forever more. Amen.

SATURDAY

O Lord God omnipotent, I ask You by the Precious Blood, which gushed forth from the sacred side of Your divine Son, Jesus, in the presence and to the great sorrow of His most holy Mother, deliver the souls in Purgatory and among them all especially that soul which has been most devout to this noble Lady, that it may come quickly into Your glory, there to praise You in her and her in You through all the ages. Amen.

Our Father. Hail Mary. Eternal rest grant unto them, O Lord, and let perpetual light shine upon them. And may their souls and all the souls of the faithful departed, through the mercy of God, rest in peace. Amen.

An Act of Contrition

O my God, I am heartily sorry for having offended Thee, and I detest all my sins, because I dread the loss of heaven, and the pains of hell; but most of all because they offend Thee, my God, Who are all good and deserving of all my love. I firmly resolve, with the help of Thy grace, to confess my sins, to do penance, and to amend my life. Amen.

An Act of Mercy for Souls
Suffering in Purgatory

Immaculate Mary, Mother of Mercy, who saw the sacred body of Your beloved Son raised on the Cross, looked at the soil soaked with His Blood, and were present at His cruel death, we offer you, most Holy Mother, the souls suffering in Purgatory, and we beg you to be so kind as to look upon them with your merciful eyes and ask for their release from their torments. In order to receive your forgiveness, O Immaculate Mother, we sincerely and heartily forgive all those who have insulted us, and through your intercession, we beg Jesus to grant them every goodness, grace, and blessing in exchange for the wrong they did to us or wished upon us. Through your hands, O Holy Virgin, we offer to the Lord this act of love, asking His mercy for the souls that are being purged. Amen.

Prayer Before a Crucifix

Look down upon me, good and gentle Jesus
while before Your face I humbly kneel and,
with burning soul,
pray and beseech You
to fix deep in my heart lively sentiments
of faith, hope, and charity;
true contrition for my sins,
and a firm purpose of amendment.
While I contemplate,
with great love and tender pity,
Your five most precious wounds,
pondering over them within me
and calling to mind the words which David,
Your prophet, said to You, my Jesus:
"They have pierced My hands and My feet,
they have numbered all My bones."
Amen.

The *Mater Dolorosa*

Words attributed to the Sorrowful Mother of God, speaking to her Divine Son when He was taken down from the Cross and placed into her arms.

O Font overflowing with truth, how wearied Your countenance.

O Wise Physician of human souls, how silent You remain.

O Splendor of Eternal Light, how lifeless You are.

O Sincere Affection, how deformed Your once beautiful
    face has become.

O Most High Divinity, in what poverty You show Yourself.

O Love of my heart, how immense is Your Goodness.

O Joy everlasting, O Love of my heart, how excessive must have
    been Your grief.

My dear Jesus, who is one with the Father and Holy Spirit,
being one and the same Divine Nature, have pity on all living
creatures, and especially for the suffering souls in Purgatory.
Amen

Five Apostles' Creeds
One Hail Holy Queen
One Our Father, Hail Mary, Gloria

Eternal Rest grant unto them and let perpetual light shine upon them. May they rest in peace.

We adore thee, Piteous Cross, adorned with the delicate members and Precious Blood of our Lord and Savior Jesus Christ.
We adore Thee, O God, nailed to the Cross who bleed for love of us.

My Jesus, by the sorrows Thou didst suffer in Thine agony in the Garden, in Thy scourging and crowning with thorns, on the way to Calvary, in Thy Crucifixion and Death, have mercy on the souls in Purgatory, and especially on those that are most forsaken; do Thou deliver them from the terrible torments they endure; call them and admit them to Thy most sweet embrace in paradise. Amen.

Seven Offerings of the Most Precious Blood

These prayers are all about invoking God's mercy for souls, especially the suffering souls.

O Heavenly Father! Have mercy on all Suffering Souls in Purgatory, for whom Thine only begotten Son came down from Heaven and took human nature to Himself. For the sake of this Thy Divine Son, pardon their guilt and release them from punishment.

1. **Eternal Father!** I offer Thee the merit of the Precious Blood of Jesus, Thy well-beloved Son, my Savior and my God, for my dear Mother, the Holy Church, that she may enlarge her borders and be magnified in all the nations of the earth; for the safety and wellbeing of her visible head, the Sovereign Roman Pontiff; for the cardinals, bishops and pastors of souls, and for all ministers of Thy sanctuary.

Glory be to the Father, etc.

Blessing and thanksgiving be to Jesus: Who with His Blood has saved us!

2. Eternal Father! I offer Thee the merit of the Precious Blood of Jesus, Thy well-beloved Son, my Savior and my God, for peace and union among all [those who govern], and for the welfare of all Christian people, [all those of good will], and [the good of society].

Glory be to the Father, etc.

Blessing and thanksgiving, etc.

3. Eternal Father! I offer Thee the merit of the Precious Blood of Jesus, Thy well-beloved Son, my Savior and my God, for the repentance of unbelievers, for the uprooting of heresy, and the conversion of sinners.

Glory be to the Father, etc.

Blessing and thanksgiving, etc.

4. Eternal Father! I offer Thee the merit of the Precious Blood of Jesus, Thy well-beloved Son, my Savior and my God, for all my kindred, friends, and enemies, for the poor, the sick and wretched, and for all those for whom Thou, my God, knowest that I ought to pray, or wouldst have me pray.

Glory be to the Father, etc.

Blessing and thanksgiving, etc.

5. Eternal Father! I offer Thee the merit of the Precious Blood of Jesus, Thy well-beloved Son, my Savior and my God, for all who, this day, are passing to the other life; that Thou wouldst save them from the pains of Hell, and admit them quickly to the possession of Thy glory.

Glory be to the Father, etc.

Blessing and thanksgiving, etc.

6. Eternal Father! I offer Thee the merit of the Precious Blood of Jesus, Thy well-beloved Son, my Savior and my God, for all those who love this great treasure, for those who join with me in adoring it and honoring it, and who strive to spread devotion to it.

Glory be to the Father, etc.

Blessing and thanksgiving, etc.

7. Eternal Father! I offer Thee the merit of the Precious Blood of Jesus, Thy well-beloved Son, my Savior and my God, for all my wants, spiritual and temporal, in aid of the Holy Souls in Purgatory, and chiefly for those who most loved this Blood, the price of our redemption, and who were most devout to the sorrows and pains of most holy Mary, our dear Mother.

Glory be to the Father, etc.

Blessing and thanksgiving, etc.

Glory Be to the Precious Blood
Glory be to the Blood of Jesus, now and forever, and throughout all ages. Amen.

Litany of the Most Precious Blood of Our Lord Jesus Christ

As you say these prayers invoking the Lord's mercy through His Most Precious Blood, keep in mind that this is the Blood that sustained St. Bridget on her journey home to the Merciful Father, and it is the same Blood that sustains us, too, through the Holy Eucharist. Indeed, it is the Most Precious Blood that pleads God's mercy for the Holy Souls. It points to the precious communion with God that they long for, which will be fully theirs when they reach Heaven and partake of the Marriage Supper of the Lamb.

So, take time each July, the month of the Most Precious Blood, to remember the suffering souls, especially at Holy Communion and in pleading the Most Precious Blood for them through these prayers. As the suffering souls themselves told St. Bridget, we, the Church Militant, can aid them if we wish; we can hasten their union with God. What a privilege and what a duty! "Glory be to the Blood of Jesus: now and forever, and throughout all ages. Amen."

Lord, have mercy. *Lord, have mercy.*
Christ, have mercy. *Christ, have mercy.*
Lord, have mercy. *Lord, have mercy.*

Christ, hear us. *Christ, hear us.*
Christ, graciously hear us. *Christ, graciously hear us.*

God the Father of Heaven, *have mercy on us.*
God the Son, Redeemer of the world, *have mercy on us.*
God, the Holy Spirit, *have mercy on us.*
Holy Trinity, One God, *have mercy on us.*

Blood of Christ, only-begotten Son of the eternal Father, *save us*
Blood of Christ, Incarnate Word of God, *save us*
Blood of Christ, of the New and Eternal Testament, *save us*
Blood of Christ, falling upon the earth in Agony, *save us*
Blood of Christ, shed profusely in the Scourging, *save us*
Blood of Christ, flowing forth in the Crowning with Thorns,
                                                    save us
Blood of Christ, poured out on the Cross, *save us*
Blood of Christ, price of our salvation, *save us*
Blood of Christ, without which there is no forgiveness, *save us*
Blood of Christ, Eucharistic drink and refreshment of souls,
                                                    save us
Blood of Christ, stream of mercy, *save us*
Blood of Christ, victor over demons, *save us*
Blood of Christ, courage of Martyrs, *save us*
Blood of Christ, strength of Confessors, *save us*
Blood of Christ, bringing forth Virgins, *save us*
Blood of Christ, help of those in peril, *save us*
Blood of Christ, relief of the burdened, *save us*
Blood of Christ, solace in sorrow, *save us*

Blood of Christ, hope of the penitent, *save us*
Blood of Christ, consolation of the dying, *save us*
Blood of Christ, peace and tenderness of hearts, *save us*
Blood of Christ, pledge of eternal life, *save us*
Blood of Christ, freeing souls from Purgatory, *save us*
Blood of Christ, most worthy of all glory and honor, *save us*
Lamb of God, who taketh away the sins of the world,
spare us, O Lord.
Lamb of God, who taketh away the sins of the world,
graciously hear us, O Lord.
Lamb of God, who taketh away the sins of the world,
have mercy on us, O Lord.
Thou hast redeemed us, O Lord, in Thy Blood.
And made us, for our God, a kingdom.

Let us pray.

Almighty and eternal God, Thou hast appointed Thine only-begotten Son the Redeemer of the world and willed to be appeased by His blood. Grant, we beg of Thee, that we may worthily adore this price of our salvation and through its power be safeguarded from the evils of the present life so that we may rejoice in its fruits forever in Heaven. Through the same Christ our Lord. (Amen.)

Purgatory Board

You may want to use the Marian Fathers' "Purgatory Board" to pray for a different group of departed souls each day. (The particular groups of souls designated for each day are listed on PrayForSouls.org.) There are 50 different categories of departed souls in all, and we Marians post in our houses one category of souls to be remembered each day — going through all 50 on a rotating basis. The different groups of departed souls include parents, benefactors, popes, bishops, priests, leaders of nations, and those who are forgotten or neglected.

1. For the souls of all the faithful departed.
2. For the souls of your departed parents and family.
3. For the souls of your departed friends.

4. For the souls whose memory has vanished from this world.
5. For the souls that suffer the greatest torments.
6. For the souls of those who died unexpectedly or without receiving the Holy Sacraments.
7. For the souls of those who died in war.
8. For the souls of those who died of epidemics or famine.
9. For the souls that shall be delivered from Purgatory this very hour.
10. For the souls that have been long detained in Purgatory.
11. For the souls that did not give proper honor to our Lord.
12. For the souls that need most prayer.
13. For the souls of those who persecuted you in your lifetime.
14. For the souls of those who did not assist others in their need.
15. For the souls of those who long lived without forgiving their enemies.
16. For the souls of those who showed great love of neighbor.
17. For the souls of those who did not give proper honor to Our Lady.
18. For the souls that are in great need of assistance.
19. For the souls that undergo severe torments for their sins against chastity.
20. For the souls that suffer in Purgatory because of me.
21. For the souls of those who suffer for having engaged in sinful conversations.
22. For the souls of those who were particularly given to mortification and penance.
23. For the souls of consecrated religious who followed the rule in a very zealous way.
24. For the souls of those who valiantly gave witness to their faith before others.
25. For the souls of sinners who have become lukewarm.
26. For the souls of those who received the Holy Sacraments rarely or with indifference.
27. For the souls of those whose bodies lie in non-consecrated ground.
28. For the souls of those whose bodies lie in your neighborhood cemeteries.

29. For the souls of those who prayed little.
30. For the souls of those who suffer for having been deliberately inattentive during prayers.
31. For the souls of those who suffer for giving bad example to others.
32. For the souls of those that leave this world this very moment.
33. For the souls of those who die a disgraceful or tragic death.
34. For the souls that are in need of the Church's prayer because they committed a sacrilege or showed disrespect toward holy objects.
35. For the souls that had a special devotion to the Most Holy Sacrament.
36. For the souls that had a special devotion to the Immaculate Conception of the Most Blessed Virgin Mary.
37. For the souls of those who contributed to the conversion of sinners.
38. For the souls of those who suffer because of their unyielding and arrogant attitude toward others.
39. For the souls that atone for their disregard for legitimate authority.
40. For the souls of those who suffer for having slandered, libeled, or told calumnies of others.
41. For the souls of those who sought their own excessive pleasure and luxury.
42. For the souls of those who died regretting their sins but without making atonement.
43. For the souls of the leaders who neglected their duties or abused their power.
44. For the souls of those who worked for peace in the world.
45. For the souls of those who contributed to the growth of priestly and religious vocations.
46. For the souls of those who dedicated themselves to the education of the youth in piety.
47. For the souls of those who supported missionary works.
48. For the souls of the Marian Fathers and Brothers.
49. For the souls of all consecrated religious.
50. For the souls of popes, bishops, priests, and deacons.

Marian Press pamphlets on Purgatory

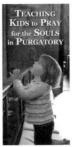